RETAIL REVELATIONS

Strategies for Improving Sales,
Margins, and Turnover

rev•e•la•tion (rĕv′ə-lā′shən) *noun*
1. a. The act of revealing or disclosing. b.Something
revealed, especially a dramatic disclosure of something not
previously known or realized. c. A sudden insight or idea.

To Max and Morgan

Retail Revelations
Strategies for Improving Sales, Margins, and Turnover

Copyright ©2015 by RMSA Retail Solutions and Ritchie Sayner
All rights reserved.

Book design by Jennifer Cassou

Published by Mizzou Publishing, The University of Missouri Student Center,
911 E. Rollins St., Columbia, MO 65211

Published in the United States of America. No part of this book may be used or
reproduced in any manner whatsoever without the written permission of the publisher.

ISBN 978-1-616600-482-8

Printed in the United States of America

Contents

◆

Foreword

◆

Retail business has never been harder. We all use many resources in retail to help us make the best decisions possible: Consultants, peers, professionals, memberships, personal research and more. You will find this resource to be the most focused and concentrated compilation of retail business articles anywhere. Think of any retail business question you have ever had. Chances are you will find a reference to it here.

A resource like Sayner's compilation of retail business articles covers virtually every topic you have ever had a question about: Metric analysis, inventory performance, personnel, staff meetings, retail relationships, buying with a plan and a purpose, marketing, customer service, management, hiring...the list goes on.

I have worked with Ritchie Sayner and RMSA for many years. His knowledge and business relationships have greatly contributed to two of our family's three generations in retail.

This book takes the place of a decade long retail magazine subscription. *Retail Revelations* is a personal library reference that you will keep on the top shelf of your bookcase-if not in your briefcase.

Randy Brown
Brown's Enterprises

About RMSA

R MSA has been in the business of helping retailers for over 60 years. Thousands of independent retailers have counted on RMSA to  help increase sales and cash flow using our proven merchandise planning and open-to-buy solutions.

RMSA clients get access to a team of retail professionals who work with them every month to ensure inventories are in balance across every category in every store. We employ a hands-on approach and build long-term relationships with our clients because we deliver a peace of mind when it comes to a retailer's biggest asset, their inventories.

The RMSA team has always taken pride in being a great educational resource to our clients. The selected articles in this book represent years of insights from working with retailers of all stripes and address issues all retailers face.

For more information on RMSA, please visit our website at www.rmsa.com or contact us at info@rmsa.com or 800-727-7672.

Thanks,
RMSA Retail Solutions

Prologue

◆

Back in 2004, I wrote a "Letter to the Editor of *Shoe Retailing Today* magazine, at the encouragement of Bill Boettge who at the time served NSRA as its president and CEO. That simple letter was the starting point that, over the past ten years, evolved into more than fifty published articles, which together make up the contents of this book.

The ideas compiled in this volume come from my own experiences as a buyer and merchandise manager, as well as from some 13,000 client reviews I have conducted since 1980 as a retail consultant with RMSA Retail Solutions.

Though some articles contain specific references to shoe retailing, they were never intended to be limited to the footwear industry. It is my hope that all independent retailers who take the time to read this book will come away with an idea or two that will help them with their business.

For people who are new to retailing, I am confident this compilation will prove a valuable reference. I often tell new store owners, "Read one or two articles a day and in a month you will know what has taken me a lifetime to learn." For seasoned retail professionals, the book is a good review of best practices.

Improved Inventory Turn Is Possible—and Essential

Editor's Note: SRT *received the following comments in the form of a Letter to the Editor from Ritchie Sayner, vice president of business development at RMSA, the Riverside, CA-based company which provides merchandise planning assistance. .*

Having studied the recent NSRA *Business Performance Report*, several areas immediately struck me that should be of major concern to the shoe retailing industry. Perhaps of primary significance would be "Retailer Priority #2" from the survey of Top Seven list of retailer priorities for 2004: **Improve inventory control/turn.**

Given the fact that the "typical" NSRA store has a sales volume of $809,000, operating expenses of 44.5% and an inventory turn of two according to the BPR findings, it should come as no surprise that cost-related issues dominate the retailer priority list. Noticing that improvement of turn did not top the list leads me to believe that several NSRA stores may not be aware of the multitude of positive economic ramifications that exist when turnover improves, including greater bottom line and/or more for the owner in salary.

I would like to suggest that increased turn is not only entirely possible, but essential if the industry is to maximize its true profit potential. The benefits that faster-turning stores enjoy are numerous and include the following:

- **Increased sales volume** (Priority # 1). A balanced assortment of inventory consisting of a constant flow of fresh new goods delivered in the correct amounts and at the correct time is the single best defense against lost customers.

- **Improved margin** (Priority #3). Markdowns erode margin. The main cause of markdowns is buying more than a store can profitably sell. Stores that turn faster take fewer markdowns as a percentage of sales than slower-turning stores, which are forced to take higher than normal markdowns to clear aging inventories and create cash to pay bills.

- **Improved cash flow** (Priority #4). Suffice to say that if the store is carrying a lower average inventory and generating the same or in most cases more sales, cash flow will be stronger.

	Typical NSRA Store	Store with 2.5 turns	Store with 3 turns
Sales	$809,000	$809,000	$809,000
G.P.%	46.5	46.5	46.5
GP$	$376,185	$376,185	$376,185
Turn	2	2.5	3
AI @r	$404,500	$323,600	$269,667
AI @c	$177,171	$141,737	$118,114
GMROI	1.72*	2.65	3.18

- **Reduced expenses** (Priority #6). Operating expenses are expressed as a percent of sales. Operating expenses drop in percent as sales go up. Since expenses for shoe stores are at a four-year high, an improvement in turnover with a corresponding sales increase reduces expenses.

My experience in working with shoe retailers is that even given the nuances of shoe retailing including sizes, widths, prepacks, delivery problems, etc., a 2.5-to-3-time annual turnover is entirely possible. I believe that one of the main reasons that faster turns are not being achieved is that shoe retailers accept the false premise that because the industry continually reports an "average" turnover of 2 historically, that if they turn twice all is well in the world. This line of thinking stymies the industry from growth by accepting mediocrity as the benchmark for which to aspire. In an attempt to think outside the (shoe) box if you will, the following example illustrates the effect that increased turn has on inventory investment and GMROI.

The results detailed on the previous page are being achieved by shoe stores today that approach their sales and inventory planning from the bottom up and at the classification level. The reduction in average inventory alone could in effect add to the bottom line as well as to the owner's compensation. Perception becomes reality and changing the perception of what is "OK" in terms of turnover is long overdue in the footwear industry. If the example provided above were to become the norm, the statement in the BPR confirming the possibility of "succeeding very profitably in the independent retail footwear business" would ring even more true than perhaps it does today.

Misplaced Priorities?

◆

The *2006-07 Business Performance Report* [makes] it evident that the independent shoe merchant is continually striving to improve, change and grow. Several instances can be seen where shoe retailers are once again reaching new heights. There is, however, one glaring example of where very little improvement has been made: inventory turnover!

In fact, according to NSRA statistics, turnover has seen little improvement since that first NSRA conference held in 1914. Turnover ranges have remained in a range from 1.8-2.1 for nearly a century. My contention is that if the independent truly understood the positive financial ramifications associated with increased turnover, this area of concern would rank #1 on the list of retailer priorities instead of a distant #3.

Increasing sales volume ranks at the top of retailer priorities. It seems apparent, based on the *BPR*, that volume is being driven by markdowns. Initial markup is at record high levels and markdowns of 23.6% are at their highest point in the past 25 years.

One interpretation of this is that the independent shoe retailer is, to a degree, "buying the business." By that, I mean taking high initial markups, then aggressively discounting product to entice the customer into the store. Unfortunately, this strategy did not result in higher maintained markups, since that particular benchmark remained unchanged this year at 46.5%.

A constant flow of fresh new merchandise properly timed, well presented, and fairly marked will provide the sales increases so coveted by today's shoe retailer. The key to faster turnover is proper merchandise planning, to achieve balanced inventories with goods purchased in the right quantities and received at the optimum time. Rare is the customer today who enters a store in search of what came in six months ago, which is [what if offered by] the store that turns its stocks twice annually.

In 1914, [NSRA's Board of Directors shared meeting minutes with the membership that contained the following advice]: *"You want to keep your stock fresh. You want to turn it three times a year. You want to be open for new stock every season that comes along. People want new goods most generally and they don't want this dead stuff."*

NSRA's advice from 92 years ago is still valid today. The retailers that push the turnover envelope will achieve the volume and margin increases that they perceive as more significant priorities today.

October/December 2006

Inventory Variance:
Take It Seriously

◆

With the holiday season behind us, now is a good time to review the past 12 months and evaluate both quantitatively and qualitatively the areas of your business that have worked well—in addition to those areas that could stand improvement.

Most retailers take a physical inventory in conjunction with their fiscal year's end. Certainly this is a recommended practice from an accounting perspective. From an operations standpoint, the benefits of a clean and thorough physical inventory are numerous. If, for example, a physical count is taken once a year and the inventory levels in the computer are adjusted and "cleaned up" to reflect the recent count, logically there will be no time in the year when the inventory reports will ever be more accurate and up to date. One of the more significant reports to generate after the inventory is reconciled is the inventory variance report. Most point-of-sale systems have one. This report reveals the differences between **book** and **physical** inventory. Book inventory is what the computer says you have on a given date; physical inventory is what you just counted and actually have in the store.

In my dealings with independent shoe merchants over the better part of the past three decades, I have found that most assume a very casual approach to inventory adjustment. This runs the gamut from the nonchalant retailer who merely accepts the difference and moves on (what I refer to as the "Oh well, it is what it is" approach), to the operation that looks into every missing sku in an effort to tighten up the operation and prevent further discrepancies.

Monitor at Both Levels

Book and physical inventory should be monitored at the store and classification level. Several things can cause a disparity between these numbers. Certainly if the previous year's inventory was inaccurate, then even if this year's count is spot-on there could be a substantial difference. Markdowns that were not properly recorded are another potential problem area to check into, assuming the store is operating under the retail method and markdowns are tracked. Transfers between stores are where a multitude of problems tend to occur as well. It is not uncommon to find one store showing shrinkage and another store coming up with an overage by the same amount. The solution here is an obvious one: Tighten up the transfer process. Discrepancies can also arise from goods being received into the wrong classifications when the merchandise arrives. If purchase orders are filled out properly, with correct department/class information, this too can be held to a minimum going forward. Missing tickets and human error at the point of checkout is another cause of inventory variance. I am continually reviewing classification information from independent shoe retailers and almost always see a class described as "unknown" or "missing." I have seen extreme examples where sales in these classes can be some of the highest volume classes in the store. It should go without saying that there shouldn't even **be** a classification in the store to track unknown or missing merchandise. To keep the merchandising information credible, **all** sales must be put into a classification when sold.

Another area for shrinkage is theft, both internal and external. Having said that, I can almost assure you that I will get emails from merchants who will claim they have never heard of this happening in their stores. Remember, just because you aren't aware of something doesn't mean that it hasn't or can't happen. There isn't a retailer on the planet that hasn't had some experience with theft, with the possible exception of the new store that has been just open for one day—and frankly, I wouldn't bet on that scenario.

Set a Shrinkage Goal

According to the NSRA's most recent *Business Performance Report*, independent shoe retailers consider improved margin and inventory control as high on their list of concerns. That being so, a respectable shrinkage goal would be anything less than two percent. Inventory shrinkage is a component of cost of goods sold (COGS), along with purchases, freight in, alterations, trade discounts earned and the difference between beginning and ending inventory. So if a store's year-end shrinkage is high, the COGS will be higher and the gross margin will be reduced accordingly. Recently, I have suggested that several of my clients begin using inventory shrinkage as one of the components of manager bonus programs in an effort to illuminate the importance of closely monitoring this area of potential loss.

In severe cases, inventory shrinkage can alter open-to-buy numbers, thereby creating a potential shortage of inventory which could lead to missed sales, a Number One priority among NSRA merchants and most certainly an area to be avoided.

As you embark on the year-end introspective ritual of looking for areas of improvement, don't overlook inventory variance. It just might be the difference between being profitable and being very profitable.

January/February 2007

Initial Markup: Your Formula
Must Meet Your Goal

---◆---

One question I am repeatedly asked by shoe retailers is how to increase maintained margin. The most obvious answer that comes to mind is to avoid overbuying and therefore reduce the margin-eroding markdowns that accompany such a practice. Another way of increasing maintained markup is to find ways to increase **initial markup**.

Let's make sure we are all speaking the same language. When I say "initial markup," I am referring to the markup percentage placed on the goods when they are received from the manufacturer. "Maintained markup" is what is left after taking into account the cost of the markdowns. Stated a little differently, "maintained markup" is the difference between net sales and the gross cost of the merchandise sold. "Gross margin" is the difference between **net** sales and the net cost of the merchandise sold. Total merchandise costs include the cost of the goods, freight inward, any workroom costs, and any adjustments for earned discounts. It is clearly a different number than maintained markup.

Initial Markups on the Rise

According to NSRA's *2006-07 Business Performance Report,* initial markups for independent shoe retailers reached an all-time high in 2005, coming in at 56.8%. This represents a 4.8 percent increase since 2001. My hunch is that the almost 5- point gain in five years is due to stores seeking out and taking advantage of off-price opportunities to combat the effects of discounters and increased operating expenses. Whatever the reason, we can all agree that initial markups are on the rise...and it's a good bet that they aren't going to go down any time soon.

Having the correct initial markup is the cornerstone to achieving the desired maintained markup. But have you ever wondered what the determining factors for initial markup are? Why do we double the cost? What does the term "keystone markup" mean and where did it originate? I'll admit that my quest for the origin of "keystone markup" did not yield any definitive answers, but it did offer some thought-provoking theories. One source at the National Retail Federation (NRF) seemed to think that there was an actual "markup key" in the early days of cash registers. This practice predated individually ticketed items and pricing was oftentimes handled at the point of sale. One expert thought the term began in the jewelry business. Another believed the phrase more closely follows the dictionary definition of the word, which is a stone at the top of an arch that locks the other pieces in place. I suppose this makes sense, since 50% of a keystoned item is cost and the remaining half is markup. Regardless of origin, keystone pricing refers to a percentage markup applied to a product's cost, although it is becoming an outdated term due to rising markups.

What Initial Markup Must Cover

In my work as a retail consultant, I routinely ask retailers to define **their** initial markup. The answers are quite interesting, and run the gamut from doubling the cost and adding $1 or $2 dollars to a multiplier of 2.2 or 2.3 as an example. These answers over time have led me to the conclusion that most retailers truly can't explain what initial markup (IMU) was intended to cover.

There are three areas that IMU must satisfy:

1) desired net profit

2) operating expenses, and

3) markdowns.

Outlined below is a formula for determining initial markup given the objectives above.

IMU = <u>desired net profit % + operating expense % + markdown %)</u>
<u>100</u> + the markdown %

Example: Let's say that our net profit goal is 7%, operating expenses are 40% and markdowns are 18% of sales. Our formula would look like this:

$$\text{IMU} = \frac{7\% + 40\% + 18\%}{100 + 18\%}$$

Using the formula, the IMU% would have to be 55% to cover the markdowns, pay the overhead and still contribute 7% to the bottom line. If the store average is, say, 52% on average, net profit would decrease to 3.4% right from the start, according to the example above. If you do the math, that is nearly a 50% reduction in profit. To restate the message, initial markup is directly related to net profit. You must start with enough markup in the beginning in order to have to something left at the end.

Review Pricing Practices Regularly

It is a good practice for all stores to review pricing practices on a regular basis. Competitive pressures, changes in operating expenses and availability of promotional goods all come into play when deciding on a markup goal. Are you making markup decisions based on what a product will sell for, or on what you paid for it? One way to avoid falling into the trap of cost-based pricing can take place when buyers are at market. The best time to determine what the actual selling price will be is at the time the order is written. In my earlier retail career, I would often have our buyers decide what they thought they could sell a certain item for, prior to knowing the cost. Once we knew the cost, we would make a decision to buy or bypass the item. Basing the retail price around the intrinsic value of the merchandise, instead of on its cost, helped us to increase our initial markup. It's a strategy that could work for your store as well.

March/April 2007

The Buying Diamond: The First Step in Assortment Planning

◆

Let's assume that things in your store are running pretty smoothly. Sales volume is growing, margins are good, inventory turnover and cash flow are fine, and operating expenses are within average norms. Good job so far—you've got the easy stuff done. To fine tune the operation and maximize the true upside profit potential, you must understand and incorporate assortment planning.

What is assortment planning?

Once purchases have been made and merchandise has been delivered and placed on the selling floor, the three questions left to be answered are:

- Will the merchandise selection properly reflect the customer's wants and needs in both price and taste?

- Will there be enough new merchandise to keep customers returning?

- Will the goods be bought deep enough to be meaningful without undermining store profitability? Some items will be fashion leaders, while other styles will be expected to contribute the bulk of the volume and profit.

Assortment planning is the a matter of determining, before purchase orders are written for an upcoming season, exactly what the merchandise selection will consist of, how it fits in to the store's markup and profit goals and how it will be presented to customers within price and taste levels. Having vendor, classification, subclass, style, size, and price point

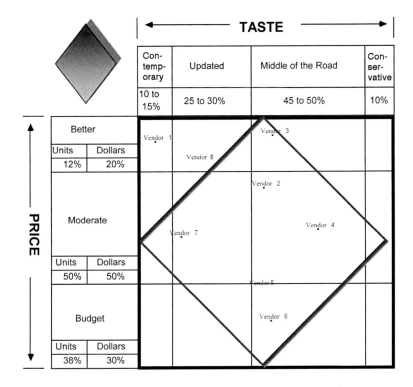

	Con-temp-orary	Updated	Middle of the Road	Con-ser-vative
	10 to 15%	25 to 30%	45 to 50%	10%

TASTE →

PRICE

Better		
Units	Dollars	
12%	20%	

Vendor 1
Vendor 8
Vendor 3
Vendor 2

Moderate		
Units	Dollars	
50%	50%	

Vendor 7
Vendor 4
Vendor 5

Budget		
Units	Dollars	
38%	30%	

Vendor 6

information available for the analysis is vital. And working with a Buying Diamond makes it easier.

What is a "Buying Diamond"?

A Buying Diamond is a visual display of what the store is selling. It is a tool to relate the two main issues always faced in making buying decisions: "Price" and "Taste." The challenge continually facing the shoe retailer is how to blend the two.

"Taste" is generically identified as one of four: "Contemporary," "Updated," "Middle of the Road," and "Conservative."

"Price" is generically identified as "Better," "Moderate" and "Budget."

What is considered as "Better" in one store might be considered "Budget" in another store. The same principle applies to "Taste": "Contemporary" in one operation might be called "Middle of the Road" in another.

The Buying Diamond is a visual approach to the planning of the proper merchandise mix. Without such a system in place to plan purchases beyond the dollar open-to-buy, a retailer runs the risk of selecting merchandise which may not completely meet the wants and needs of the store's customers. In addition, an assortment that has not been carefully planned may very well be unbalanced with regard to taste level and price points. Lost sales and excessive markdowns can very easily be the result of *not* carefully planning assortment planning.

How does the Buying Diamond work?

The basic premise of the Buying Diamond utilizes a grid with the "Taste" components across the top and the "Price" components on the side.

Taste Level

The "Taste Level" portion of the planning process can be viewed as the fashion cycle, with the newest looks entering under "Contemporary" on the left, then moving to the right and ending up with "Conservative." Over time, fashion moves from left to right as you face the Buying Diamond. A merchant will always want to have some vendors in the upper left area of the diamond. Doing so assures that the retailer is well positioned when trends turn into hot sellers. This type of merchandise is generally purchased in the better price points, since the customer looking for it is forward-thinking and usually looking for innovation and technology. If the new looks fail to move, the first markdown will generally move the merchandise into an acceptable price point for the store.

Price Points

The "Price Point" section breaks prices into three levels. Usually a store can adequately cover only three price point ranges without confusing its customers and spreading its open-to-buy too thin. As a general rule, 20% of the purchases are allocated to "Better" goods, 50% to "Moderate" and the remaining 30% to "Budget." The middle 50% will achieve the store's average gross margin, the bottom 30% will most likely provide the highest gross margin and the top 20% will most likely be the least profitable.

Once the price points have been established, the vendors are placed on the chart in the taste/price area most representative to their lines. A diamond is then super-imposed over the vendor selection. Vendors falling outside of the diamond will undoubtedly not perform as well. The farther away from the diamond a vendor is, the more likely higher markdowns will result.

Email for Detail

The Buying Diamond originated with Paul Davidow, a veteran retailer and former colleague who has since passed away. He used it very successfully, and unselfishly taught it to others. The retailers I work with who use it do so with satisfaction and to their profit.

_____

May/June 2007

Develop a Productive
Market Strategy

◆

With the August WSA Shoe Show about to open, this is perhaps a good time to discuss market strategy. Based solely on personal observation, far too great a number of retailers do very little, if any, pre-market planning. For sure, there may be some appointments made with vendors ahead of time, but that is not what I mean by planning.

Markets take time and resources away from the store for days at a time in some cases, and while admittedly it can be exciting to see fresh new offerings at first hand, visiting a market is no time to waste time. Decisions will be made that you will have to live with for perhaps the next six months, making this a time to pay attention to business.

Pre-Market Planning

Prior to attending any market, it is important to meet with your buying staff. Participants should be prepared to discuss vendor performance, including sell-through, profitability, shipping, promotional allowances, etc. If a vendor has *not* produced at an acceptable level, this is the meeting to formulate a plan for dealing with the vendor, since decision-makers usually attend major trade shows.

The store's open-to-buy should also be discussed, so that buyers know what the budgets will be for a given class of merchandise. Open-to-buy (OTB) plans for the upcoming season should be reviewed and finalized so that, pending any major fashion shifts, buyers have a good idea of how much to spend by store and classification.

Six Steps to More Productive Markets

Pre-market plan – Develop your plan before you leave.

Cover expenses – Find off-price goods to cover market expenses

Shop other retailers – Look at how other stores handle things, to give yourself new perspectives.

Look for new lines – Always leave enough time to see something that you don't already carry.

Shop by classification – Organize appointments by classification whenever possible.

Hold a wrap-up session – As soon after the market as possible, bring everyone involved in buying to a wrap-up session, where you can review, make commitments and reallocate as needed.

Make the Trip Pay for Itself

It is also a very good practice to challenge every buyer to find enough opportunistically priced merchandise (off-price goods) to at least cover their individual market expenses (travel, lodging, food). If you encourage buyers to go to markets with the caveat of finding enough "deals" to cover their expenses, rarely will you be disappointed. This idea can pay huge dividends—and it can sharpen a buyer's focus.

Show Time

Some stores like to spend the first day of a show getting acclimated to what's going on. They like to "walk" the show, get a visual of trends, check out new lines that might look interesting, talk to old friends, and otherwise give themselves an overview experience. I think this is a healthy practice.

It is also a good idea to have buyers check out other retailers when traveling on business. Look at the lines other stores are carrying, and how the goods are displayed; check signage; evaluate sales personnel. You won't be able to help but compare your operation to those you are visiting, and you're almost sure to get some new ideas.

Don't Overbook

Most retailers have preset market appointments with their major vendors. Be careful, however, not to get yourself so overcommitted that you leave no time to look for new vendors to test. Remember, the constant flow of fresh new product is what keeps customers coming back—fresh product produces sales increases, which in turn improve turnover and cash flow.

Look by Classifications

Another market strategy that is useful is to organize your buying into major classifications whenever possible. Larger stores can afford to have separate buyers for each product classification. In the majority of independent shoe stores, buyers buy it all. Shopping by classification helps make it easier.

For example, if you are shopping for athletic shoes, winter footwear, and women's dress shoes at a particular market, buy them in classes independently if possible. Schedule appointments when previewing dress shoes to look at as many dress shoe lines as you feel you need to in your price range. Try not to confuse the issue by looking at a dress shoe line, then going to a boot resource, then seeing an athletic shoe company, then back to a dress shoe line. Shop your dress shoes, then move on to your boot lines, then preview your athletic shoes vendors. You will make better buying decisions—and avoid duplication—by using this strategy to stay focused.

I am not a proponent of "leaving paper" at market. In making that statement, I know I am risking bodily injury, not to mention the emails that are sure to come from reps telling me what they think of my opinion. However, that being said, I hold firm to the premise that leaving orders in a show room without having seen all of the other lines on your shopping list is a surefire way of getting overbought, having duplications, and ending up with too many markdowns at season end.

After Market

A market recap held at the conclusion of the show, or shortly after returning home, with *everyone* involved in the buying decisions is a good practice. Everything you have just seen will still be fresh in your minds. Open-to-buys and assortment plans can be reallocated as needed; new lines and trends can be finalized, and commitments made.

If you commit to embracing the above market strategy, I am convinced you will be able to maximize market time and expense. Try it, beginning with the upcoming show—and enjoy a more productive market experience.

_____

July/August 2007

Understanding
GMROI

◆

Wouldn't it be great if there were a way to improve your profitability without having to increase sales **or** margins? I know the idea sounds like one of those commercials that promise you will lose weight without diet or exercise, but it happens to be true.

What's the magic answer, you ask? It is: "Understanding the concept of GMROI." GMROI is short for Gross Margin Return on (Inventory) Investment. It is calculated by taking the gross margin of a store, department, classification or vendor and dividing it by the average cost inventory for the same period. For every dollar invested in inventory at cost, how many gross margin dollars are you getting back?

> **Increased Turns=Increased Cash Flow**
> An improvement of only 1 week in annual sell-through increases cash flow by approximately 1% of annual sales

Should $1 Yield 87 Cents?

Would you be willing to invest $1 knowing you were only going to get back 87 cents on a given style, a particular vendor, or in a classification of merchandise? I certainly hope not, yet some stores that do not understand the impact of GMROI allow this to happen season after season and year after year without taking corrective action.

Consider the chart to the right. The sales, COGS (Cost of Goods Sold) and gross margin number are the same for all three examples. The only component that has been changed is the turnover. The first column illustrates the discussion above of investing $1 and getting $0.87 in return. Column 2 is representative of the average NSRA store according to the *2006-2007 Business*

Performance Report. Column 3 shows the effect an improvement in turnover can have on cash flow and GMROI. The $0.35 improvement in GMROI amounts to 19.2%. Where else can you achieve such a significant increase in profitability? This is, in most cases, a best of both worlds scenario: Improve cash and profitability while at the same time spending less.

Effect of turnover on average inventory investment

Annual sales volume: $1,000,000
Cost of Goods sold %: 53.5%
Gross Margin: $465,000

Turnover	1.	2.1	2.5
Weeks' supply	52	24.7	20.8
Average Investment at Retail	$1M	$476K	$400K
Average Investment Cost	$535k	$255k	$214k
Cash improvement		$280k	$ 41k
GMROI	**$0.87**	**$1.82**	**$2.17**

Turns Hasten Improvement

Assuming that the gross margin is not uncharacteristically low, improving turnover is the simplest and quickest way to improve GMROI. Margins have been relatively stable since reaching a record high in 2003, so it seems evident that there is not much opportunity for upside growth. The opportunity that is available to the independent shoe merchant is one of increased turnover.

What never ceases to amaze me in discussions with independent shoe merchants is how some can agonize over how to control expenses. Let's use freight costs, which might run about 1.5% of sales, as an example. The freight costs have retailers wincing—yet the same retailers are relatively complacent about a storewide inventory that turns twice annually.

As the chart illustrates, an improvement of just four weeks of supply on average inventory would generate about a 4% improvement in cash flow. This slight improvement would cover the freight costs for nearly three years. So—which area really deserves the most attention?

If you desire an increase in GMROI, then it is vital that you find ways in which to improve turnover. I will be happy to share my thoughts on improving turnover with anyone who wishes to email me about this.

Breaking the
Non-Profit Cycle

◆

A common frustration that I often hear among retailers is: For all of the long hours, hard work, new ideas tried, and innovative merchandise purchased, profits don't seem to change much from year to year. Stores that experience little or no gain in annual profits may find themselves victims of the **non-profit cycle**.

Just what is a non-profit cycle?

It's a cycle often found in retail operations where no merchandising information exists from which to base buying decisions. In other cases, some level of information may be available—but due to data integrity issues or incorrect merchandise planning procedures, a solid merchandise plan fails to be developed. Figure 1 shows an example of the non-profit cycle. Notice that the cycle progresses in a clockwise direction, with each event building on previous problems. Poor planning or—worse yet— **no** planning typically puts stores in an overbought position. True, an argument could be made that under-buying might result, but in the shoe retailing

Figure 1

world, where the aggregate turnover is 2.1, according to NSRA's *Business Performance Report*, buying too little clearly isn't the problem.

Overbuying leads to higher average inventory and therefore to slower turnover. When turns slow, cash flow is negatively affected. Poor cash flow leads to vendors not getting paid on time, which in turn causes incorrect timing of merchandise in the form of late or partial shipments. Now we have a store that has no balance to the inventory, which affects sales. As sales decline, bank loans are sometimes considered as an option to pay vendors. Markdowns that are above normal are generally next in this scenario, due to the fact that too much was purchased to begin with or was received late. In severe cases, markdowns may be needed to generate sales volume to cover the loan payments.

Overbuying Raises Other Costs

As if this isn't bad enough, when stores buy more than they can profitably sell, they pay higher operating expenses than more profitable stores. Here is a partial list of operating expenses that could rise due to overbuying: rent, advertising, payroll, taxes, insurance, interest, supplies, credit card costs, freight in, and market expense.

Let's look at these expenses individually. If you pay percentage rent and you are selling goods at reduced prices, you end up generating low-margin volume that you will pay rent on. In a sense, you are "buying the sales" with markdowns. In this scenario, the landlord and the vendors are the only folks who make any money, not the retailer. Advertising typically needs to be stepped up to generate the traffic; taxes and insurance are also above the norm on stores carrying more than they need. Expenses—such as bags, boxes, wrapping paper, order forms, office supplies, phone costs, and signage—all rise when a store overbuys. Would you rather pay the credit card discount points on an item that you sold at full margin, or one that you just marked down to cost? Remember the loans taken out to pay the vendor? Interest on bank loans and/or personal credit cards will also get added to the profit and loss statement. Freight expense on merchandise that is now not needed becomes yet another cost, especially if it's being sold at half price. How about the time spent at market viewing extra lines and buying merchandise that ends up being sold at a loss? Although I could continue, you get the point.

Breaking the Cycle

All of this leads to little profit—or no profit whatsoever. The reason that the cycle is so difficult to break is the fact that retailers have short memories. In planning for next year, it is common to mistakenly look only at what happened last year. Armed with the

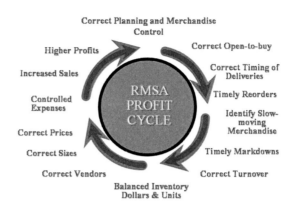

Figure 2

misconception that planning for a decrease generates a decrease (or other misguided ideology), an increase in sales is often projected, albeit unwarranted. More planned sales volume translates into more inventory, which slows turnover, and so the cycle continues.

The Profit Cycle

As the name implies, the Profit Cycle is a more desirable pattern in which to operate (see Figure 2). In this scenario, the merchant has good merchandise planning procedures and buys correct amounts of inventory that are delivered at the right time. Reorders are identified early on "hot" sellers and markdowns taken on "dogs." When the inventory turns the proper number of times and deliveries arrive as scheduled, inventory balance improves. Assuming that proper assortment planning has been done (see "The Buying Diamond," *Shoe Retailing Today*, May-June 2007) with regard to vendors, sizes, and prices, one might expect expenses to be under control and sales volume to increase, generating higher profits.

As with many things in life, only when a problem is recognized is corrective action ever considered. If you find yourself continually operating in a non-profit cycle, you can change the situation. It's a matter of first identifying the cause of the problem and then implementing a solution.

Developing an Ongoing
Marketing Strategy for Growth

◆

Part of being prepared is to have a marketing strategy that will help you achieve your merchandise performance goals. The concept of creating an ongoing marketing strategy for your business is certainly not new. However, in working with retailers, I have found that too often there is disconnect between the customer's needs and the buying, visual presentation and marketing plans for your store.

There are three questions that can help you develop an ongoing marketing strategy that positions your store for growth:

- What are your customers looking for?

- What will make my merchandise appealing?

- What is my marketing strategy?

What Are Your Customers Looking For?

To get that answer, the first questions you may want to ask are, "What does my customer expect from me?" and "Why should they shop in my store?" The best way to identify the answers is to ask your customers. There are a variety of techniques that you can use solicit this information, including surveys, letters, postcards, one-on-one contact, point of sale inquiries, etc. Pick a method that feels comfortable, and start asking.

Your goal should be to find out what factors of the shopping experience are most important to your customers: merchandise selection, key trends, important vendors, value, price-points, customer service, or a simple explanation of why they buy the merchandise that you have selected for them.

Once you have identified your customer's preferences, you can determine your store's specific trends and what merchandise will meet customers' needs. Use this information, along with your open-to-buy plans, to create specific merchandise buying and assortment plans. Remember that while it is tempting to want to accommodate each individual request, it's a better strategy to focus on the desires of the majority of your customer base. By doing so, you will know how to best distribute your inventory investment dollars to appeal to your customers, and thus, improve your sell-thru and turnover.

What Will Make My Merchandise Appealing?

Once you have identified key customer preferences and purchased merchandise accordingly, the next step is creating a visual presentation of merchandise in your store that customers will respond to. From the front windows to the back walls of your store, have you identified your most profitable merchandising areas? Are the colors right? Are the most important trends featured in the best positions, with less trendy items towards the back? Are your display walls appealing and visually strong enough to attract customers?

Regular visits to the sales floor to evaluate merchandise presentation are critical to determine if the merchandising execution matches your vision for the displays. A quick check of sales figures will tell you if customers are responding to merchandising by making purchases. If not, what needs to be changed? Should you re-merchandise more often during this most important time of the year? Is the newest merchandise always prominently displayed? Are you providing add-on selling suggestions by displaying coordinating items together? For example, you can show how to accessorize a look, or display related items not normally merchandised together.

What Is My Marketing Strategy?

Now that you've identified what your customers want and created compelling displays of merchandise, you are ready to think about your specific marketing plan. How will you take all this information and use it to build a plan that will bring your customers into the store? Marketing activities should be designed to meet two purposes: building customer loyalty, and generating sales.

There is a wide range of ideas that can be considered to set your store apart from everyone else: direct marketing, customer loyalty programs, invitation-only shopping events, in-store special events, fashion shows, "how-to" seminars, vendor or trunk shows, trade magazine advertising, in-store signage, in-store music, personalized follow-up letters to customers...just to name a few.

It's Not Too Late to Plan a Great Season!

Many of you have already made a plan and are prepared to put it in action as the New Year begins. If you **haven't started** your planning, be assured that it is not too late! Use these ideas, or new ideas of your own, to start building a plan that will make the most of the season in your store.

Always remind yourself, "What are the compelling reasons why my customers shop in my store?" It seems like a simple concept, but with the demands placed on retailers today, the simple things sometimes get overlooked. I hope this article helps to generate new energy and discussion that will enable you to have a very prosperous new year.

_____

January/February 2008

How to Improve Cash Flow

◆

Let's begin with one simple multiple choice question:

Which answer below helps to improve cash flow?

A. Reduce expenses
B. Increase sales volume
C. Improve inventory turnover
D. Raise maintained markup
E. Properly timed deliveries
F. All of the above

If your answer was "F," congratulations—you are probably a savvy retailer. Cash is King in the retail business. Strong, positive cash flow is a must for any thriving retail establishment. The benefits of positive cash flow are numerous: pay vendors on time, take discounts, expand or remodel, add brands, pay yourself more, and so on.

Poor cash flow forces retailers to make survival decisions they may otherwise not make. This is what I commonly refer to as *Management by Crisis*. Decisions made during periods of difficult cash flow might include not taking discounts, paying vendors late, paying COD for inventory, not taking entrepreneurial risks that might be good for the business, cutting back on essential services that keep a healthy business thriving, bank loans taken out when needed cash is sitting in boxes on the shelves, and running sales events out of panic in order to create cash, to name a few.

Let's look at ways that cash flow can be improved.

Reduce Expenses: Make sure that operating expenses are in line with industry norms. NRSA's *Business Performance Report (BPR)* is a great benchmarking tool for this. Set an operating expense budget based on current volume and stick with it. Two of the largest and most common areas that get out of line are occupancy and payroll costs. However, if you are continually borrowing money to finance a heavy inventory, you are probably paying unnecessary interest expenses.

Increase Sales Revenue: More sales at the register mean more cash in the bank, assuming that the sales are being generated at normal margins. Excessive markdowns taken as a result of overbuying or other merchandising infractions are not considered a profitable way of generating sales. Effective use of off-price merchandise can be a vital component to driving volume.

Improve Inventory Turnover: Since this topic has been covered previously in this column in prior issues, suffice it to say that reducing the average inventory and not buying more than you can profitably sell is essential to keeping cash flow positive. Understanding GMROI (*page 22*), which blends average inventory and gross margin would be very useful here.

Raise Maintained Markup: Increasing maintained markup can be accomplished by either raising initial markup or reducing markdowns. NSRA reports in its *BPR* that average initial markups now top 56%. Since this is an average, not all stores need this high of a markup, while others may need more. Good retailers maximize IMU wherever possible. This is the reward for diligent buying and good negotiating. In today's retail environment, all retailers need to strategically avail themselves to opportunistic pricing (buying off-price) whenever possible in order to maximize maintained markup.

Properly Timed Deliveries: The timing of merchandise deliveries is critical to the optimization of cash flow. This point is closely linked with all of the points previously covered. What sells fastest in your store, the new merchandise that arrived just ahead of the new season or last season's leftovers that you couldn't even get rid of on sale? If vendor terms aren't pre-arranged, some stores end up paying for goods months before they have had an opportunity to sell them in some cases. I have also seen examples of stock levels in seasonal categories (i.e., sandals or winter footwear) that are actually higher in the months following the season than they were during the season, due to accepting late deliveries.

Since inventory is most often a retailer's single largest asset, more time and resources should be devoted to monitoring this area. Accurate sales and inventory forecasting is essential in order to maintain and strengthen cash flow. Consider two simple facts. First, inventory related costs take over half of a retailer's annual budget (the NSRA average = 53.5%, according to the *BPR*). Second, operating expenses eat up over 40% (the NSRA average = 43.1%, according to the *BPR*). In other words, $.96 of every dollar is committed to merchandise and expenses when things are running normally. When items A-E above are the least bit out of sync, cash flow begins to erode. Most prudent people wouldn't think of not having insurance on their home or car for peace of mind and protection. Think of a comprehensive merchandise plan coupled with a cash flow plan as an insurance policy for your largest asset: your inventory.

———————

March/April 2008

Off-Price Buying:
Strategies and Pitfalls

◆

M any shoe retailers spend more time planning their vacations than they do planning their inventory.

Of course I can't prove that, but it stands to reason given the fact that the average shoe store still turns inventory twice annually and is accepting of a GMROI of less than $2.

If we accept as fact that proper inventory planning is a key component to maximizing profitability, it makes sense that more time spent planning would lead to increased profits. Given that 50.2% of open-to-buy dollars are allocated to initial or advance purchasing and the remaining 49.8% are spent on in-season on fill-ins and replacement orders (NSRA's *Business Performance Report 2006-07*), according to my math, that leaves nothing available for the purchase of **off-price merchandise.**

Off-price merchandise can be a significant booster of business, provided retailers understand six key aspects:

- What exactly is off-price merchandise?

- The benefits off-price offers to the retailer

- Common misconceptions

- When buying off-price works for a store

- When it does not

- Buying strategies

What exactly is off-price? Quite simply, it is merchandise made available from a vendor at a discount taken from the original line price, hence the term "off-price." In fact, off-price could be considered the markdowns that the vendor must take for reasons similar to a retailer's reasons for taking mark downs. Slow moving merchandise, and goods that were manufactured too late or not up to specifications, are common reasons. Cancellations from large retailers are sometimes a cause as well. More often than not, vendors get stuck with extra product when they have failed to forecast their customers' needs accurately.

Benefits to the retailer. When a store is able to procure off-price merchandise from a supplier, it can serve to generate several benefits. If used effectively and the product is in-season, better margins, faster turnover, and increased volume all result. If the special buy is used as a traffic builder and the "savings" passed on to the customer, a "good will" element also is generated.

Common misconceptions. From time to time, I have heard retailers say that they don't buy off-price because either they tried it once and it didn't work well or they felt that they were buying someone else's problem. Both arguments are faulty.

First, just because something was tried once doesn't mean that it won't work the next time. Several questions must be asked in order to determine if the buy was good or not. For example, how much was purchased? What was the price? Was it a good item from a vendor you usually buy from? Was the merchandise timed right? How was it marketed once it was received? Regarding the second argument, oftentimes retailers get an opportunity to buy into the very goods that they purchased originally. Other times, a popular style becomes available for any number of reasons. By its very nature, off-price buying has a certain element of risk, but so does the shoe business in general.

When it works. The benefits of off-price merchandise can best be realized when a retailer plans for the buy in advance. It is not always easy to predict what exactly is going to be available. This goes for vendors, quantities, price, sizes, colors, and delivery timing. That being said, when a retailer is in a healthy financial position and keeps open-to-buy dollars available for such buys, more often than not deals can be found. Sometimes an off-price purchase can be negotiated in advance when an initial order is being considered.

When it doesn't. If a store is overbought to begin with, buying *more* merchandise is generally not advisable, no matter what the price is. You already have your own markdowns to worry about, let alone someone else's. This would be like pouring gasoline on an already blazing fire. If you buy more off-price merchandise than your company can absorb, you will be defeating the purpose and will not be able to benefit fully from the buy. Additionally, if you buy product simply because the price is attractive yet it won't stand up to the rest of your criteria, you are doing your company a disservice. Remember, the objective is to resell this merchandise quickly and make money. If you buy based on price alone, you run the risk of getting burned.

Buying strategy. If you are one of those folks who visit the gym once every quarter, you probably don't see much value. The same applies to buying off-price merchandise. Make it part of your regular merchandising strategy.

A basic open-to-buy strategy that you might consider would be to spend 50% of your money on initial or advance orders, 30% for fill-ins and reorders and keep 20% available for opportunistically-priced merchandise. An open-to-buy plan that is prepared by month, store and classification would greatly simplify this process.

By allocating a portion of your open-to-buy dollars specifically for promotional merchandise, you will become more disciplined about seeking it out instead of waiting until it is offered to you. Be persistent in asking vendors what merchandise is available. Ask them to contact you immediately when they break price. You may not always be able to buy, but you should always take the time to look. Once you find merchandise that would be good for your store, and you have confirmed that open-to-buy dollars are available, don't be afraid to pull the trigger.

Off-price can also be used in the vendor negotiating process. This may take the form of an upfront agreement. For example, if you are buying more inventory from a given vendor than you had initially planned based on their insistence, perhaps the resource would be willing to share the markdown burden with you should the additional styles not perform at an acceptable margin or a preset sell-through is not attained. Remember that all of this is a negotiation. There are no pre-set rules and one size does not fit all.

With off-price buying, your motto should be simple: *Buy the Best, and Pass the Rest!*

The Power of New

---◆---

Which sells the best: fresh new merchandise received just in time for the upcoming season, or inventory left over from last year that you didn't clear out because you had a complete run of sizes that you thought you could sell during the next season? With even a remedial understanding of the concepts of turnover and gross margin return on investment (GM-ROI), it should be easy to determine that new goods **always** trump old merchandise when it comes down to what will sell the fastest. The longer an item remains on the floor unsold, the more it costs you—not only in real dollars, but in opportunity costs. It might be more accurate to say "in missed opportunity costs." In the past, we have discussed both turnover and GMROI in this column so I thought we could use a fresh approach to discuss *"The Power of New!"*

Early in my career as a merchandise manager, I was assigned the task of improving the sales in the shoe department of the department store where I worked. Our shoe buyer was an older man who had been in the shoe business longer than I had been on the planet and we both knew it. In the process of reviewing our falling sales and heavy inventory position with him, I convinced him that a tour of the stock room would be eye-opening for both of us.

The Stock Room Tour

And was it ever! I was looking for left-over sizes, bad colors, poor fitting models, discontinued vendors and other slow sellers that we could imme-diately slash, so we could generate cash and open-to-buy dollars to reorder fresh merchandise that was beginning to sell. **He** was proudly pointing out complete size runs of shoes that we have owned for longer than I am willing to admit in print. When I said we really needed everything on sale that had been in our store longer than six months with the exception of models that he could justify selling in the next season, he looked at me like I had two heads. After the purging was complete, our inventory had been reduced by about one third in both dollars and pairs, sales volume in the department was growing at a rate of roughly 20% per month, and margins were improving because we were selling newer goods at full price instead of out-of-season product that we were lucky to sell for "cost."

Even today, some shoe retailers are very skeptical when they hear me say that sales volume and margins can increase with a decrease in their inventory position. Did I mention that cash flow improves because new customers find their way to your store and existing customers buy more? I am currently working with several retailers in this exact situation. One merchant in particular comes to mind. The store is turning its women's shoes 3.2 times, all the while enjoying a 49.5% margin and a 15% sales increase over the last year. **Over 98% of this merchant's inventory is less than three months old.** My discussions with this store are different from others that I often have. There is no complaining about the poor economy, how $4.00 per gallon gasoline is keeping customers from the stores, what the competition is doing or which vendors didn't ship this or that. Instead, we constantly review current fast-selling models for possible reorder and slow sellers that can be reduced in season with a small markdown. Remaining open-to-buy dollars are used for off-price goods to add freshness to the assortment and bolster the margin. *The Power of New* has changed this retailer's total approach to his business.

Merchandising the New Versus the Old

Grocery retailers generally have a greater understanding of *The Power of New* goods than shoe retailers do. That shouldn't be surprising; they have to, otherwise they must throw their inventory away—literally. Next time you are in your neighborhood grocery store, look at how the bananas are merchandised. Typically, the newer fruit has a bit of green on the tip. These are the bananas that will be perfect to eat for the next few days. On the other hand, the old bananas have already begun to show their age by virtue of the dark spots on the skin. These will soon be bagged and discounted as their value to the store is diminished as their value to the store is diminished and their only remaining purpose is to become banana bread.

The point is that no-one comes in to your store purposely looking for old merchandise, unless they are solely bargain hunters. Shoppers, especially women, frequently show stores looking for what is new. Prove *The Power of New* to yourself. Change a display in your store, rearrange a fixture or redo the window and see what happens. Items you may have had for a while will begin to sell because they appear "new."

Address It Now

Here's a money-saving tip that can help you now. Identify anything in your store that is more than six months old. What percentage of your inventory does this represent? If more than 20% is older than six months, you have a potential problem. If over 30% of your stock is old, it is no longer a "potential problem"—it **is** a problem that needs to be addressed now! Mark it down and clear it out! Reorder items that are selling well and search for promotional inventory if your open-to-buy will permit.

Put *The Power of New* work for you and watch your sales and profits increase.

_____

July/August 2008

Turnover: Big Improvement, But More Needed

◆

Two years ago, an article appeared in this magazine that I wrote entitled, "Misplaced Priorities?" The essence of the article was that if inventory turnover were given more focus by shoe retailers, the other concerns—of increasing sales volume, improving margins and strengthening cash flow—would, in effect, self-correct.

Fast Forward

Fast forward to the present. It appears that many of you have taken what I said in 2006 to heart. According to NSRA's *2008 Business Performance Report*, the typical store's inventory turnover has jumped from 2.1 to 2.4 times annually. This represents not only the largest increase in turnover ever reported for a given period, but also the highest the number has ever been. What I surmised would happen if turnover improved didn't turn out exactly as I stated, though. I was expecting to see margins as well as volume increase as a by-product of increased turn. Margins did improve, volume did not. Gross profit percentage increased from 46.5% to 48% on average, but average sales per location dropped 7.2% from $897,320 to $832,635.

Good News

There is good news, however, if you read between the lines. Due to the fact that initial markup jumped 0.6% to 57.4% and markdowns came down 1.6% to 22%, overall gross margin climbed to 48%, its highest point ever. But wait, there's more. Since turnover increased because average inventory at cost went down by nearly 21%, GMROI jumped up from 1.81 to 2.19, a respectable 21% increase. Net profit also came in nearly 20%

above 2006 levels, to add one more positive point. Greater inventory efficiency yielded higher profits, both in percentage and in dollars.

The bottom line is that several shoe retailers are doing a better job of selling what they have and no longer are buying into the adage of "the more you have, the more you will sell,"—at least, so it appears.

One possible explanation for the decrease in sales reported in 2007, while margins and turns improved, might be that retailers may have in fact been "buying the business" as I mentioned back in 2006. On average, some of you may be selling a little less, but are keeping more of what you do sell. Any financial planner will tell you it is not how much you make, but how much you keep that is important.

Lesson from History

On May 19, 1913, *The New York Times* ran an article about a study that Harvard had conducted on the shoe trade. What Harvard's researchers discovered was that "stock was staying in shops too long" according to the headline. The article went on to predict that "increasing turnover(s) would swell profits without raising prices." That may have remained true if operating expenses had not risen since 1913, nor had the initial markup needed to cover them. Prices did rise nearly 4% in 2007, but improved turn has strengthened both cash flow and net profit.

Dramatic Upswing

In the 2006 report, 16% of responding stores felt that improving turnover was their third highest priority. By 2007, the number had swung dramatically to 41%, giving "improving turnover" a solid #2 ranking, an indication that retailers are becoming convinced of the benefits of faster turn.

In 1913, shoe retailers were advised that turning stocks three times would insure maximum return on their inventory investment. I, for one, plan to keep beating the turnover drum until the 3X goal as set forth 95 years ago is attained and turnover becomes the top merchandising priority of the independent shoe retailer.

_____

Starts and Stops NOW: Take Advantage of a Tough Economic Climate

◆

Most of life is habitual. We tend to do the same things we did yesterday, the day before and every day for the last month and the last season. In retail, habits—good **or** bad—make your store what it is. The key is controlling them. If you recognize what behaviors need to be changed, then even a small effort can create big changes.

There are **five things you need to STOP doing right now!**

1. Stop blaming the economy or competition.
How is it that some retailers thrive and grow in a down economy or in the face of fierce competition? The answer is, they don't let the economy or competition dictate how they operate their businesses. In tough economic times, these retailers pay attention to what made them successful in the first place. They leverage their strengths and eliminate their weaknesses. And they take steps to enhance and improve their relationships with their customers. Service is a *huge* opening for the independent retailer. The big boys are understaffed, underpaid and underknowledged. And they are constantly losing touch. Successful retailers understand that the economy and competition are out of their control. What is **in** their control is the ability and desire to make their store the best that it can be.

2. Quit ignoring the obvious.
If there are fewer customers coming through your doors today than last year, re-evaluate your advertising and marketing. If the average sales transaction is decreasing, re-evaluate your sales training techniques. What incentive plans have you put into place recently to reward your sales force?

Be Prepared for the Shows

To prepare yourself for shoe shows, consider the following tips:

- Know your OTB by month. Don't buy more than you need because of minimum quantities. Always ask yourself how long it will take to sell what you are buying. If the answer is more than 3 or 4 months, you may be asking for trouble. And walk the show before you place any orders, to get an overview of the products offered. Don't decide too quickly.

- Never spend more than 50-80% of the OTB. Save the remainder for in-season deals and opportunities.

- Look for items that jump out at you just as they would for your customers. Pretend you are your customer, and look for items that are really unique and special.

- A digital camera is a great tool. Many shows will tell you that you cannot use a camera, but it is ultimately up to each vendor. If they know you, they will let you take pictures.

- Use your own purchase order forms, not vendor forms—and never give an order without a cancel date, typically no more than 30 days after ship date. Every order should clearly state delivery date and cancel date. Remember, it is easier to buy 72 widgets than to find 72 customers to buy each of those widgets.

If profits are down, re-evaluate your merchandise management approach and expense control. Significant change in the marketplace, the economy, the competitive environment, consumer buying habits, or anything else that negatively impacts your business requires a thorough re-evaluation. Retailers go out of business because too often they didn't adjust their strategy when things first started to change. Be objective, be realistic and tackle problems head on.

3. Stop thinking of marketing and promotions as an expense.

Marketing and promotions are a necessary investment in your business regardless of the economy or other outside influences. Be pro-active. Drive the business. In 2008, doing nothing will get you exactly that in return: Nothing. And promotions don't always have to be price incentives. In-store events, fashion shows, trunk shows, giveaways...there is a long list of activities to keep your store relevant. You Tube, My Space, Face Book and even text messaging are clever ways of using technology to reach out to new and existing customers. A simple idea that too many retailers ignore is customer reward programs that encourage customers to come back and shop again. Successful retailers know that marketing, promotions and event planning are a critical part of keeping their store in front of their customers. And get your vendors to participate.

4. Stop coming to trade shows underprepared.
For most independent retailers, going to a trade show is the single most stressful event of the season. Often, just traveling to the show causes stress, especially in these days of high fuel costs and airline delays. And it is getting more expensive. Be prepared. Remember the difference between *buying* and shopping. Buying is the process we use to select products for our customers; shopping is what we do when we buy for ourselves.

Staying clear on the difference is critical. You are your customers' eyes and you should have a clear vision of what is important to your customer as you prepare to shop the show. Don't decide too quickly. There is a tendency to buy the first exciting things we see—and later, seeing even better items, we buy them, too. Walk the entire show before you start placing orders.

5. Stop overbuying.
Stop purchasing more inventory than your traffic can bear. The key for independent retailers to weather these turbulent times, and stay liquid until business opens back up, is to adhere to basic retail fundamentals. The most basic is: Buy only what you can sell profitably. In this environment, it's nearly impossible to simply sell your way out of over-bought and over-stocked situations. Many stores report that the weakness they've experienced has been primarily in traffic counts and, to a lesser extent, in units per transaction. Simple sale promotions, while incrementally driving more traffic into the stores and having only a minor impact on units per transaction, significantly reduced sales per transaction—and most significantly cut the legs out from under gross margin. Customers who were not primarily motivated by price, didn't buy more; they just paid less for what they did buy.

The key is to **keep inventory levels in line with realistic sales forecasts**. Excess inventories in a weak sales environment back up **very** quickly, which creates enormous markdown pressure. While exceptional discounts begin to move the unit inventory necessary to bring stocks into line, those markdowns destroy gross margins.

Don't Fall for Half-Truths

There are five "little white lies" some vendor reps use to shade the truth:

- "You are getting the best price." Usually, this means you are paying what every other independent retailer is paying, not what the larger customers pay.

- "This is a show special and will not be available later". Most show specials are available for up to two weeks after the show.

- "It is our best selling item." It may be best-selling to other retailers, but there is no guarantee that it is best-selling to consumers.

- "There is no problem with deliveries." At this moment, yes, but after the show when the orders are tallied, you may not receive the item.

- "You will get dating." The clock on the dating, however, often starts when they pick and pack, not when you receive it.

Vendors aren't looking to poison relationships, but when sales people are under pressure to produce, it's human nature to push the sale. Don't let yourself get stampeded.

I also strongly advise not to spend it all upfront. Many independent retailers feel they have to commit all of their dollars upfront to get the merchandise they want. It's far better to stay liquid, holding dollars back and flowing merchandise out through the season as close as possible to the time of expected sale. That way, inventories remain lean, customers are always seeing fresh arrivals, and there's cash to spend on long-margin opportunity purchases late in the season.

There are also **five things you need to START doing right now.**

1. Increase cash flow.
This should be your number one priority. In 2008, strong positive cash flow is truly a competitive advantage. Thinking about inventory in terms of time is the essential starting point in effectively managing inventory and experiencing healthier cash flows. For many retailers, thinking of inventory in terms of weeks or months of supply is a new concept. This is ironic because often retailers who can't answer the "how many weeks' or months' supply" question are the same retailers who experience recurring cash flow problems. Remember this important retail metric: For every

week you can improve your annualized inventory sell-through, you improve cash flow by approximately one percent of annual sales.

We sometimes hold on to the mistaken belief that maximizing sales will lead to maximizing cash flow. Not true. It is optimizing turn rates that ultimately will lead to a healthy cash flow and increased profit in your stores.

You can improve cash flow by doing three things right now:

- Follow your open to buy.

- Recognize mistakes and take markdowns quickly. Your inventory is more perishable than you realize. Studies have shown that as much as 80% of your sales come from inventory less than 10 weeks old. The health of your store is in direct proportion to the newness of your inventory.

- Do not let out-of-stocks of wanted replenishable items infect your merchandise mix. Make sure you have set up model stock reorder and MIN/MAX capabilities in your POS system. If you are consistently out of stock, improving cash flow becomes almost impossible.

2. Take a critical look at every expense.
This is something the best retailers constantly do. When times are good, it's easy for expenses to creep up and get out of hand. Rather than cutting costs across the board, here's a simple way to look at expenses.

Don't spend money on anything unless it does **at least** one of these four things:

- Get more customers through your door.

- Better serve your customers

- Support your associates

- Directly help grow and improve your business.

Every other expense should be carefully scrutinized.

3. Come to markets prepared.
How well you buy, how much you buy, how well you negotiate, how professional you are can make a big difference in your bottom line at the end of the year. And by all means **go to market**. Staying home to save money is "penny-wise and pound-foolish."

Use your own purchase order, not the vendor's, as it has your own cancel date and other requirements of doing business with your store. The vendor form is built in their favor, not yours.

Narrow the shipping window. An order that comes in between August 1 and October 31 is unacceptable. Make sure that every order clearly states delivery date and a cancel date no more than 30 days after the scheduled delivery date.

4. Start negotiating.

More than ever before, both landlords and manufacturers are willing to work with their independent retail customers, with whom they have a history and good credit in the marketplace.

Many retailers are holding back on opening additional stores at this time. We have seen downsizing, bankruptcies, and major retailers not only **not** adding new spaces, but actually closing stores. Vacancy rates are up. Traffic is down. Landlords have fewer candidates for their vacant space. As a consequence, independent retailers who do want to open stores have less competition and are able to get more affordable rents, better locations or both. Today independents are successfully negotiating advantageous new leases, lease renewals, rent reductions and spec reductions.

If you are experiencing any difficulties, now is a good time to renegotiate your lease. If you **aren't** experiencing any difficulties, now is also a good time to try—you might get better terms if your landlord fears having another untenanted space.

If you have cash on hand, remember that vendors need cash, too. Talk with them about what they can offer you in exchange for cash. And remember: They can't deliver to retailers who aren't making payments—but they still need to move merchandise. There may be good deals available if you take the time to look for them.

Try to get as much as you can when you are preparing to buy. Remember, the vendor is never more accommodating than when you are standing there with your pen (or cash) in hand. A few things to negotiate for:

- 60+ day payment terms—plus 30-day terms from the day you receive the merchandise, not the shipping date

- Pre-paid shipping

- No pre-approval for damage/defective returns and full refund (not credit note)

- Co-op advertising

- Guaranteed repeats

- Free goods for display

- Guaranteed sales—90 days

Write on all orders "No Backorder" so that you move up the ladder on shipping priority.

If your credit is good and you have a history with the vendor, you will be surprised at how successful you can be. Remember: The worst that can happen is, they say no.

5. Start training and incentivizing your sales force.

Many independent retailers simply don't have expectations for sales production. They say, "Here's what you have to sell this week or this month to keep your job." Essentially these retailers put people on the floor, pay them an hourly wage and hope they sell. Then there are the retailers that have some concept that people want to make more money. So they put in an incentive program and start paying commission.

The problem with that strategy on its own is that it doesn't give salespeople skills to succeed or tools to measure their progress. How people behave on the sales floor is related more to how they are trained and managed than to how they're paid.

Get everyone on your staff professionally trained. Turn your staff's "helpfulness" into high-performance selling. Set accurate and objective sales goals. Make sure your employees are making enough add-on sales. Understand the new sales metrics and how they impact sales. These are behaviors—and they require that you have weekly coaching meetings with your sales staff. Establishing esprit de corps results in better customer service and higher sales. If you invest in your people, they can become your biggest asset.

Keep learning, keep challenging yourself and your associates. Even in difficult economic times, the best retailers take bold steps to distance themselves from the competition. They continue to identify and take advantage of the opportunities that are there, even in a competitive environment and a tough economy. Retail maybe the toughest profession out there, but there's always room for those who get it right.

November/December 2008

Understanding Today's Retail
Climate—and Then Moving Forward

♦

In some ways, I think we can come to accept the current retail climate by first understanding Kubler-Ross's "Five Stages of Grief." In her book entitled *On Death and Dying*, originally published in 1969, Dr. Elisabeth Kubler-Ross pioneered methods of support and counseling during personal trauma and the grieving process associated with death. Her ideas, known as the Five Stages of Grief model, are easily adaptable to personal change and emotional upset, and don't have to be relegated to dying. The five stages are denial, anger, bargaining, depression, and acceptance. I have observed retailers dealing with the economic state of flux that we are currently living with—and many are going through a process very similar to what Kubler-Ross outlined. See if you have ever experienced any of the emotions described below.

Denial

When a retailer first notices slow business in general or items not selling as they should, *denial* is often the first emotion felt. "This can't be right," "the POS information is wrong," "I have all the right vendors and styles," and so on, are immediate reactions. "There is nothing wrong with my merchandise." In this stage, the retailer keeps plodding along, anticipating things will soon change.

Anger

Denial usually morphs into anger. I would lump "blame" into this stage, because the outlet for retailer anger can be blaming someone or something: The vendors shipped late, the fit is bad, the customers don't understand our store, the weather is too good or too bad, the landlord hasn't done anything to promote the center, and advertising isn't effective. The list of what to blame is endless. In this stage, the retailer can't deny what is happening any longer, has admitted such, is mad and is looking for someone at whom he can point the finger.

Bargaining

The bargaining phase can take many forms. Initially, re-merchandising the selling floor may prove fruitful. Changing displays gives the customer the appearance of new shipments of merchandise, often a stimulus to sales. Sometimes spiffs or PMs (push money) are the next course of action. The idea here is to provide the salespeople with an added incentive, while maintaining full price and preserving gross margin. This method can be very effective if it is not overused. Let's say you decide to give a $5 spiff on a $100 model that is slow. If effect, that is equal to a 5% markdown—which most retailers today would agree is wasted effort. Yet an extra $5 per pair in a salesperson's pocket might just work.

Vendor returns are another form of retail bargaining. This is an effective technique used to return poorly fitting styles for credit, or slow-selling merchandise for newer inventory that will hopefully sell faster. This privilege should not be abused, but is a good way to maintain margin and/or reduce stock level.

The final bargaining tool available to the retailer is of course the markdown: Reduce the price in the hope of a quick sale. You can tell that this is the last straw for the retailer—they don't want to see the merchandise again, which means a stricter return policy.

Depression

Retailer depression can itself have several levels and can be of indefinite duration. Sometimes the depression sets in after the initial response to a markdown is not up to expectation. Other times, the markdown is taken too late in the season or not deep enough to rectify the problem, leading to poor results. With all of the store doom and gloom heaped upon us by the media lately, coupled with more store closings than we have ever seen at one time, it is easy to understand how depression could set in.

Acceptance

Once a retailer accepts the current situation whatever it may be, he or she is now ready to move forward. That will involve resolving not to let themselves get into the same situation again—by planning better, buying smarter, being more aggressive with vendor returns, canceling late shipments, or being quicker with markdowns. Now the retailer is truly at a point where he or she can move forward rationally and positively, hopefully having learned from the experience.

Perhaps you have recognized this cycle or portions of it in yourself. If you are experiencing, or have experienced, some of these stages, you are normal. The problems arise when we get stuck in any one phase for an extended period time and can't find a way to quickly move into the final stage of acceptance. In reaching acceptance, most retailers find it helpful to speak with someone outside of immediate family or coworkers. Accountants, bankers, trade associations, and retail consultants are oftentimes helpful in identifying the real cause of the problem and mentoring the store in finding satisfactory solutions.

Many business leaders think that, in hard times, they need to put the company on their own shoulders, call the shots, create a survival strategy, and personally execute it. But recent research suggests that, instead of "hogging the ball" during tight economic times, great leaders get help from others. They listen to employees and customers, they seek out fellow business leaders, they talk to people who understand their company.

This option is typically more cost effective by far than continually going it alone—which often nets less than favorable results. When you network with colleagues, you almost always get a new perspective, which can lead to new ideas and solutions. In this economic climate, we need to talk—and listen—carefully to each other. As we network, we strengthen our ability to adapt—which, in tough times, is essential.

January/February 2008

Classification Merchandising:
Keeping Up with Trends and Budgets

◆

Most retailers today use some sort of structure by which to assimilate, organize and analyze sales and inventory data. The term used to refer to this process is "classification merchandising." Although the importance of classification merchandising was recognized decades earlier, it wasn't until the mid 1960s that its usefulness came into vogue. Practical applications got jumpstarted when retailers began using computers to crunch raw data to create sales and inventory reports.

By definition, a classification is a "natural, separate, and distinct grouping of merchandise within a department." Items in a classification must be kindred, meaning that they would all have the same end use, similar markup and turnover goals, as well as like selling patterns. Sometimes classifications and departments are referred to interchangeably, although this is not actually correct.

Dollar Control

Classification merchandising is not to be confused with unit management or assortment planning. It is a dollar control process. Information needed to render a classification system usable includes sales, receiving, price changes, transfers, returns to vendor, inventory, and merchandise on order.

Dress shoes, casual shoes, boots, sandals, and accessories are all examples of potential classifications. Let's look at "boots" as a classification more closely. Certainly there are several types of boots. Western boots, for example, are completely different from winter boots, which are altogether different from hiking boots, which are not the same as work boots. Sales volume or percentage of sales in each area would most likely dictate if classifications require separate designation. In certain situations, "boots" might actually be a department split typically by gender, such as:

Dept. 1—Boots-Women

Class 1A Women's western boots

Class 1B Women's winter boots

Class 1C Women's hiking boots

Class 1D Women's fashion boots

Avoid Generic Classifications

Combining all boots into one generic classification should be avoided as it would render the data useless, due to the differing end uses of the products, sales cycles and turnover rates. The only time this should be considered would be if store volume in this area didn't warrant further breakdown.

Dollar open-to-buy plans are controlled at the class level. Fast-selling classes should always be awarded open-to-buy even if other classes are overbought. While sales gains in a given class justify expansion of the class or reordering hot selling styles, a declining sales trend is cause for corrective action—which might include markdowns, order revisions, vendor returns, spiffs, or remerchandising of displays.

Classifications over time become trendable and predictable. Winter boots typically sell from September to a fashion customer on into January and February to the sale customer. This cycle is repeated every year, more or less, depending on variables including weather, merchandise assortment, and economic factors.

Common mistakes in classification merchandising include "robbing Peter to pay Paul," not remaining consistent, being over-classified, and treating brands as classifications.

It must be human nature for buyers to want to rob Peter to pay Paul, which means funding the overbuying of one classification with dollars from another classification. This is wrong on several levels. First, classifications are individual revenue centers in a store; they are autonomous. A buyer who would attempt to justify overbuying a boot classification by taking money from, say, the casual class is similar to a grocery store buyer ordering too much bread and having no budget left for bananas. It just doesn't work that way. If the boot class needs more open-to-buy, based on expected sales trends, anticipated "hot" items or new vendors, then the boot classification plan should be revised to adequately compensate for the additional business that is expected. Taking money from another class runs the risk of diluting the class and missing potential sales.

Consistency Is Key

A pitfall in classification merchandising is not remaining consistent with your categories. Avoid the temptation to call something a casual shoe one season and a similar item a dress shoe the next. Another problem occurs when a style is purchased in a particular classification and, once received, ends up in a totally different classification. To solve this dilemma, a store should use its own purchase orders with class numbers clearly visible. This will eliminate any confusion when goods are received and ticketed.

Create clearly defined classifications and adhere to them. That is not to say that categories cannot be split, combined, or eliminated, or new ones added as business trends warrant. Classifications should typically be reviewed at least annually. I have seen several examples of stores having so many classifications that any reports generated are useless. Computers are a great help in gathering data, but when setting up a classification system remember the adage, *need to know vs. nice to know*. Computer systems today are so powerful that an over- classified store ends up with data that is never used. It becomes akin to drinking from a fire hose. A well designed classification structure should separate the trees from the forest, but not the leaves from the trees.

Avoid setting up a class structure by brand or vendor. Planning at the class level is initially done prior to buying for the season. Creating an open-to-buy plan by brand lends itself to all sorts of problems. One significant issue develops when a class is trending up and the brand is trending down. If an increase is planned for a given brand and it is later determined that the current season's line didn't warrant an increase, the reality is you have no plan. Hot vendors can cool and weak vendors can become important. Class history, however, continues from year to year and readjusts based on your customers' purchasing trends. Planning at the vendor level is a function of assortment planning, not classification planning.

Open-to-Buy: No Secrets, but Lots of Sense

---◆---

Given the current state of retail, a business acquaintance suggested recently that I write an article about open-to-buy (OTB) planning. My original reaction was, "Who wants to read about that?" However, a review of previous articles for *Shoe Retailing Today* shows that I have covered many things **but** open-to-buy. Since I work for a company that provides independent retailers with open-to-buy plans, I guess it might be about time.

I am going to let you in on a trade secret: The formula for OTB is not difficult. Begin with planned sales, determine the first-of-month inventory level, factor in markdowns, transfers, and vendor returns, add in merchandise receipts, subtract what is on order and whamo! You have your OTB. Simple...or is it?

Let's start with *planned sales*. Where do they come from? Most independents get into trouble right out of the gate by getting this segment of the planning process wrong. A common, albeit incorrect, approach is to plan monthly sales volume based on last year. Using last year's figures to project future sales is wrong on several levels.

What Drives Sales?

If sales last year were driven by markdowns and were thus unprofitable, there is a good chance that planning around that number for the upcoming year may render the same—if not worse—results. If sales were off due to a downward fashion trend or poorly timed shipments, the classification would also falter and the store may in fact end up under-planning the classification. Sales planning, projecting, forecasting or whatever label you wish to assign to it needs to be done at the classification level and not by brand (*page 52*). Most independents almost always want to plan for an increase in business whether warranted or not. An unrealistic sales forecast will generally lead to an overbought situation, which in turn will lead to increased markdowns at best and decreased turn and cash flow at worst. Classifications get planned up based on **profitable** sales and trends, and down when the reverse happens. Merchandise planning that originates at the class level and rolls up to the department and onto the store level is referred to as bottom-up planning—as opposed to top-down planning that emanates from a total company plan and works its way down to the class level.

Planning the needed stock level to support the sales plan is the next phase. This is accomplished by the use of stock/sales ratios. A stock/sales ratio is simply a relationship between stock and sales. It is related to the turnover and the proper timing of deliveries. Stock/sales ratios are different for each classification and for every month. This is perhaps the single most compelling reason for automating the planning process.

For example, a classification that is planned to turn three times would have a s/s ratio of 4/1. This can also be viewed as the number of months of supply to have in stock.

(In fast numbers, that's 12 months/3 turns = 4 months of supply.) If a classification holds more than it can sell for a given period of time, the stock/sales ratio increases and, over time, turn will decrease. In severe examples, this can lead to higher markdowns than usual, reduced margins and an overall reduction in GMROI (gross margin return on investment) as well.

Current Retail Value

Getting the inventory planned correctly is a vital step. When using the retail method of accounting, as we are in this discussion, stocks are planned at the **current retail value**. This means that markdowns are recognized when they are taken, as opposed to when the merchandise is actually sold. This reduces the "market" value of the inventory by the amount of the markdown, which increases turnover and generates additional OTB dollars to land new merchandise. Some systems do a much better job at handling this than others; you can trust me on that.

So far we have discussed the two most important elements in the creation of an OTB plan: sales and inventory forecasting. If errors are made in either of these areas, the OTB plan is going to be wrong. After planning sales and stock levels, markdowns need to be planned for. Some stores fail to do this, arguing that the additional inventory planned to compensate for the markdowns leads them to become overbought. I would argue the reverse. By not planning for the markdowns, the classification can become under-stocked and thereby miss potential business—and who wants to risk that? Store history can help us with the planning of markdowns. Traditionally, seasonal classes like sandals and winter boots show heavier markdowns toward the end of the selling season. Knowing this, we can plan our buys around this to take advantage of promotional goods for these expected "sale" periods.

Other components that must be recognized are merchandise transfers in and out and vendor returns. Once these are properly accounted for, we now have our gross planned receiving at retail. This number can readily be converted to cost for stores that prefer buying at cost, as opposed to retail using the cost compliment of the initial markup of the classification.

Subtract On-Order from Planned Receiving

Our final step in OTB planning is to deduct what is already purchased by month of planned delivery. Once the merchandise-on-order is subtracted from the planned receiving figure, you have your open-to-buy number. Simple, right?

OTB plans are typically done for a season, say spring or fall, and generally, though not always, in six-month increments, depending on the commitment requirements of the particular classification. A good planning program is not static. It should revise itself monthly, based on the rate of sale in each classification, amount of markdowns needed or taken, and other factors. A good rule of thumb for our current economic climate would be to consider spending no more than 60% of the season's OTB up front, reserving 20% for fill-ins and 20% for promotional buys. This is a guide only, and will vary based on type of store and the classification involved.

Results of poor OTB planning or no planning can be quite costly and generally lead to inventories that are out of balance. Under-planned classifications lead to lost sales, whereas over-planned categories typically end up less profitable due to markdowns and slower turnover. Attention also needs to be given to reporting accuracy, since inventory variance can substantially alter the merchandise plan. The capture of markdowns and transfer reporting is a good first place to look if you encounter an inventory variance that is outside of industry norms.

Not using an open-to-buy plan is like driving a car without insurance or building a house without a blueprint: dangerous. Sometimes the outcome can be disastrous.

May/June 2009

Do You Need to
Generate Cash NOW?

◆

Problem: Your accountant tells you that you have a net profit of, say, $50,000, but your bank account says the exact opposite. And you feel pressure to start generating cash now.

It is, unfortunately, a not-atypical retail scenario, one that occurs way more frequently than you might expect. It's helpful to analyze the situation and see what options you might consider if this is happening to you.

Clara Peller made a name for herself in the mid-1980s doing commercials for Wendy's hamburger chain, when she asked, "Where's the beef"? The above scenario is the same idea, but let's call it "Where's the cash?" A quick study of the two viewpoints shows us the same sales, the same purchases, and the same expenses. If everything is the same, why then does the accountant think you are *making money* when there is no money in the checking account?

The obvious answer is that the cash is tied up in the unsold inventory. The following questions must now be addressed:

- How did it get there?
- What can be done to get it out?
- How can you prevent the same thing from happening again?

As we can see in both examples, sales volume is the same, as are purchases and expenses. The "cost of goods" calculation takes into consideration beginning and ending inventory, whereas the checkbook shows only cash coming in and cash going out. Therein lies the problem. Clearly, this retailer is purchasing more than he is capable of selling. The extra inventory, carried on the books as an asset, adds to the net profit and is therefore taxable.

The harsh "real world" fact, however, is that the store sold a million and spent a million-fifty on inventory and expenses and is now fifty grand in the red.

Unfortunately, this is not an uncom-

Your Accountant Tells You	
Sales $1,000,000	
Beginning inventory at cost	$250,000
(Plus) Purchases	$700,000
(Less) Ending Inventory	$350,000
(Equals) Cost of Goods Sold	**$600,000**
Sales	$1,000,000
(Less) Cost of Goods	$600,000
(Equals) Gross Profit	**$400,000**
Gross Profit	$400,000
(Less) Expenses	$350,000
(Equals) NET PROFIT	**$50,000**

Your Bank Account Tells You		
Cash In	Cash Out	
	Purchases	$700,000
	(Plus) Expenses	$350,000
Sales (cash in) $1,000,000	Total (cash out)	$1,050,000
	($50,000)	

mon scenario. It is a larger problem than it has been in the past, due to the economic challenges facing retailers at present. Your "friendly banker" may not be so "friendly" now when asked for a loan. In some cases, the bank may even want more collateral in order to extend lines of credit. In the eyes of the bank, more collateral may mean more inventory, because inventory to them is an asset. And now the real fun begins.

A retailer who finds himself in this situation needs to take immediate action. The old saying that "Cash Is King" couldn't be truer than it is today. So, the first step in the process is to generate cash by reviewing all expenses and reducing and/or eliminating non-essential expenses. Examples might include renegotiating rents and reviewing payroll, typically a retailer's two most significant expenses. Secondly, contact vendors to see if payments can be pushed back an extra 30-60 days wherever possible. Thirdly, using your POS system, run reports showing which vendors and models are not performing up to par, and take action. That action could include returning goods for other merchandise in the future, returning goods for credit, marking slow movers down, or offering SPIFs to employees, to name a few possibilities.

With the dollars that will be freed up by the above actions, reorder proven hot sellers, especially in key sizes so sales don't get missed, and look for off-price goods to build traffic and margin.

To keep this scenario from recurring, it is important for the merchant to discover what caused the cash crunch in the first place. Certainly this year, the lagging economy can be blamed for part of the problem. When fewer customers are buying less, it obviously translates into lower sales volume.

I would contend that the underlying problem stems from the store's approach to sales and inventory forecasting. The answer to any of the following might uncover some flaws in the planning process:

- Are sales and stock levels planned at the classification level by store from the bottom up (healthy)—or are they planned from the top down beginning at the total company level (usually not as healthy)?

- Are sales plans retrended at least monthly and adjusted up or down based on rates of sale?

- Is there a markdown strategy in place—or are markdowns taken on an "as needed" basis when slow sellers become apparent or cash is needed?

- Are slow movers recognized and dealt with in season?

- Are deliveries actually scheduled based on when goods are needed—or are shipments allowed to come in at the whim of the vendor? Or do the shipping instructions read more like ship "*as ready*, complete *whenever*"?

- Are hot sellers identified and reordered in a timely manner?

- Are open orders reviewed on a regular basis?

- Are there open-to-buy dollars left in season to take advantage of promotional goods—or do these purchases get placed anyway while you hope for the best?

Those aren't the only questions that need to be asked, but asking them will get you focused on inventory flow, which is a critical element in cash flow.

Perhaps you recognize patterns in the above scenario that describe your business from time to time. If so, the key is to recognize it, identify the problem(s) and be proactive about finding solution(s). Problem-solving makes for good business.

Price Is Just One
Component of "Value"

◆

It is virtually impossible to pick up a newspaper or magazine, or listen to a speech, these days without seeing or hearing the word "value." Recently, I have read several articles quoting retail CEOs as saying that their customers are more "value-conscious" than ever before. "Value coupons" pop up daily in newspapers and on websites throughout the country. "Good value" is what we all want when spending our money.

What are we really saying when we talk about value?

According to my dictionary, the word "value" has several meanings. The two that are of most meaning to retailers are:

1. A fair return or equivalent in goods, services or money for something exchanged.

2. The monetary worth of something.

So what creates the "value"—or what your **customer** perceives as "value" or "added value"? In layman's terms, "value" is receiving something above and beyond for your money—simply put, getting something extra. Since the current economic climate is rapidly accelerating the consumer's mindset from his or her usual shopping behaviors toward value-based purchasing, the conscientious retailer must find ways to present value in every aspect of the shopping experience.

Product & Service, PLUS

Recently, my wife and I visited a restaurant in our community that was new to us. We mentioned to our waitress that it was our first visit. The food was good and the service was fine. We were pleased with our "purchase" and we talked about the likelihood that we'd return. When the bill was presented, it was accompanied by a package of the company's freshly baked muffins. Since it was our first visit, our waitress had wanted us to have something extra, to thank us for coming, and she said she hoped we would return soon. She provided "value"—she gave us something above and beyond what we were expecting. Although there are several restaurant choices in this particular area, her value-added service separated this one from the others.

"It's not just about deals or price," Marshal Cohen told retailers during NSRA's First Annual Conference, "it's about giving customers what they want—and what the customer wants is better value." Cohen went on to say that the new deal in selling is finding the best value—not simply looking for sales, but looking for added value on what the customer really wants.

Retailers in the past have always been able to attract customers with deep discounts. Make no mistake: There will always be a "sale" customer who buys on price alone. The new reality, however, is that there will be fewer of them. Today's customer **isn't** shopping price alone, and she demands more from the shopping experience. I periodically receive calls from store owners concerned that frequent price promoting will "train" their customers not to buy unless something is on sale. Personally, I think that bus has already left the station. The big boxes and the department stores have seen to it that any customer "training" relative to discounting has been completed. Simply pick up any newspaper in any major city on any given day if you need additional proof.

A Consistent Message

The value message throughout needs to remain consistent, regardless of whether we are discussing value in our pricing or in our customer communications. What your customer is searching for today is not much different from what you as merchants do when you go to market. Certainly price is a component, but most merchants I know are buying from resources that offer **value** in the form of dating, freight or advertising allowances, stock balancing, and trunk shows, to name just a few examples.

Value pricing originates with value buying. Call it what you will—off-price, promotional, closeouts, or opportunity buys—the point is to seek out the best deals that your vendors have to offer and negotiate your store's own "value" items. It makes sense that perhaps a greater portion of each classification's OTB be reserved for just such items. To take this one step further, instead of waiting for what might be left at season end, begin planning for these purchases at the beginning of the season. Mother's Day, graduation, Easter, Father's Day, Independence Day, Back to School, Sidewalk or crazy days, Christmas, Labor Day, and Memorial Day, as well as your store's anniversary, are all examples of events that value-priced goods should be purchased for.

When communicating with your customer, maintain and emphasize the value theme. This can be accomplished through advertising, email blasts, and direct mail when you are creating campaigns that go out to the customer; you can also carry the theme through with store signage, window displays and impact displays within the store. Don't forget that product knowledge and customer service are essential value components that help distinguish the progressive independent merchant from the rest of the pack.

Get Creative with Value

There was a time not so long ago when value meant simply marking down remaining inventory at season end. **News Flash: Times have changed for retailers—and those days aren't coming back any time soon, if ever.** The big boxes and department stores continuously market with price promotions throughout any given season. This relentless discounting has created a numbing effect similar to that of a narcotic. After a while, the consumer builds up such a tolerance to markdown pricing that deeper and more aggressive markdowns are needed to achieve the same effect. There was a time when 20% off meant something. Nowadays most customers won't walk across the street unless the discount offering is much greater.

As you fine-tune your fourth quarter marketing calendar, get creative and see what you can do to add value to your customer's shopping experience this holiday season.

_____

September/October 2009

Time for a Check-Up: Give Your Store an Annual Physical

◆

The stock market rise in Q2 of this year was due in part to companies slashing every conceivable expense and trimming excess inventory to a bare minimum. In the short run, this practice leads to increased profitability even without top line revenue growth. While trimming unneeded expenses and stock is always a prudent business move, this pathway to profitability proves short term if avenues to increase cash through sales growth are not developed at some point.

The retailers spotlighted in the case studies below have accomplished that goal. Both operations are established businesses that wanted to reach the next level, and were willing to go outside of their organizations to do so. They "outsourced" the sales and inventory forecasting function to gain an objective, independent perspective of their businesses. The process began, as it does in all cases, with a simple evaluation called a Financial Performance Review (FPR). The FPR helped pinpoint the major issues facing each of these retailers so that a custom-tailored solution could be employed. The results speak for themselves. Here are their stories.

Case Study #1:
Multi-Location Business

This particular operation is a multiple unit store. They have a good reputation in the industry and are reasonably good merchants in general. During a basic review of the merchandising numbers, immediate ways to improve cash flow became apparent. Even though the store had fairly reliable information systems, the data was not being used effectively and therefore potential benefits were not being realized. The back room was bursting at the seams with out-of-season goods and the majority of any given season's inventory was front-loaded. Attempts at open-to-buy planning went right out the window as soon as another hot line came along that they hadn't left money for. Fill-ins and promotional buys could not be financially justified, but still occurred anyway.

By initiating a basic bottom-up sales and inventory forecasting system using data they were already collecting, positive results soon became apparent. The short-term results included:

- No longer sitting on old goods

- Not driving sales volume with markdowns

- Balanced inventories between store locations and classifications

- Deliveries timed closer to need

- Closely following a sales and inventory forecast that was not based on last year, but rather on the current trend of each classification

- Reduction in the amount of pre-season buying, thusly leaving money for fill-ins, re-orders, and promotional buys.

The bottom line: Inventory is down over $1,000,000 at retail and markdowns have been reduced by over $100,000. The company has more cash available than ever before, even given the fact that sales volume is off due mostly to economic factors.

Case Study #2:
Single Location Business

This is a single location store in a small town, a second generation operation now in the midst of transferring ownership to the next generation. Upon initial interview, the obvious problem was lack of sales growth. Every response to my questions was, "That's the way we have always done it." This business was also clearly in need of a culture shift: Business practices that seemed to work for Mom and Dad in the 1980s and '90s weren't working out so well for Junior in today's retail climate. OTB was talked about only prior to major markets, and the foundation of the plan was questionable at best. Vendors were given what appeared to be an open checkbook to write initial purchase orders. When that failed to occur, the store looked at what they had purchased the previous year and placed orders from there. Markdowns, when taken, were done only in January and July. Promotional goods were rarely considered because "Dad got burned once before," the mindset being that they would be buying goods no one else wanted.

We had to work quickly and efficiently or this store was not going to make it. The merchandise classification system that was in place needed to be redefined. An inventory was then provided by classification, so that we had an accurate starting point. Future orders began being monitored regularly, and adjusted based on current selling patterns. Each classification was reviewed monthly to determine overall trends. Using the store's POS information to spot style, size and color opportunities, we were able to begin chasing hot sellers, as well as identify slow movers so that corrective action could be taken. Open-to-buy dollars are now reserved for re-orders and for **opportunistic buys** which are now part of this store's purchasing strategy.

The bottom line: Sales volume is up in double figures, margins are healthy, turnover is above industry norms and cash flow is strong. The real benefit, however, is that Mom and Dad, who are transferring ownership to their adult child through a buyout agreement, no longer worry that their lifelong work won't be around to fund their retirement, or that their "child" won't have a future of gainful employment (and a good way to support their grandchildren).

Both operations, while different in many respects, had several things in common that contributed to their ultimate success:

- a willingness to change old habits

- openness to new ideas

- receptivity to outside input

- the ability to supply the data needed to properly guide their business.

Schedule Your Store's "Annual Check-Up"

Whether your store does $500,000 in annual sales or $25 million, it makes good business sense to have an annual check-up, especially if there have been significant changes in the business in the past year. Think of it this way: If health reasons kept **you** from working in your store for a period, your business probably wouldn't be as successful. That is the very reason most responsible people have annual physicals. Applying the same logic to your business should result in fewer economic maladies to contend with—and perhaps fewer store closures for the retailing industry overall.

As we wind up what has been a challenging year for most retailers, take time to review and reflect on your business in order to see what changes should be implemented in the upcoming year. A Financial Performance Review (FPR) is a quick, easy, confidential, and best of all **free** way to determine at a macro-level your overall financial well being. By investing no more than three minutes of time and answering five simple questions, you will be able to see where you stand compared to other similar stores, what your true upside potential is, and possible trouble spots that should be addressed.

_____

November/December 2009

"Do You Want
Fries with That?"

———————————— ◆ ————————————

Most of us probably would have to admit that at one time or another we have succumbed to the fast-food drive-in experience. In case that doesn't sound familiar, I will try to jog your memory:

You pull up at a nationally known burger joint and stare at menu board, trying to figure out just exactly what will do the least amount of damage to your arteries while some barely audible kid's voice blares at you from a tin speaker. Inevitably, whatever I order, whether it is a hamburger at lunch or a cup of coffee in the morning on my way to an appointment, the follow-up query seems to be, "Do you want fries with that?" Most recently, this query has been refined to inquire as to the size of fries I might want, adding that I can be super-sized for a small upcharge. The amazing thing to me is that it **always** seems to be fries that are being pushed, even if fries don't exactly match up with my order.

I'm the type of person who would order fries if I wanted fries, so I am not a good candidate in this environment. I have to assume, however, that this strategy works for most customers, or the burger joints wouldn't continually use it. If you know the nature of retail sales people, you know that suggestive selling is a technique that must constantly be reinforced. I would assume that to **not** suggest fries is met with some mild admonishment at the very least—and with a much harsher reprimand or some equally punitive reminder at worst. The bottom line is that the margin on fries must be outstanding.

Increased Sales Volume—and Margin

The point is, suggestive selling not only works, but can add significant percentage to store sales volume and margin. In most shoe stores, shoe care products, insoles, and even socks for that matter wouldn't achieve the volume levels they hit today if not for suggestion by a salesperson. According to the National Shoe Retailers Association's 2008-09 *Business Performance Report*, sales of non-footwear items increased from 7.6% of sales to over 12% of sales between 2003 and 2007. There is even some speculation that this increase may contribute favorably to the improvement in store turnover that has been reported. I see this as a distinct possibility.

My contention is that suggestive selling, when done properly, is not only additional sales and profits to the store, but also service and therefore **value** to the customer. Inexperienced or poorly trained sales associates are happy when a customer simply makes a buying decision for a primary item. The only other decision that therefore needs to be made in their mind is method of payment. The seasoned sales person, on the other hand, sees the selling process as just beginning when the customer agrees to the shoe, sandal or boot. Socks are a no-brainer for shoes and boots. There will also be no better time to suggest shoe care products and insoles. Handbags and belts in some stores can also improve the value of the transaction.

Make It Fun

Getting sales associates to remember to offer additional items to a customer requires constant attention. Making a game out of suggestive selling can make for a lively morning meeting with the sales staff. Give the same item to several different sales people at the same time, and allow them each thirty seconds to pick up as many additional items as they can think of. Thirty seconds is about the time you have to take a customers purchase to the cash check out area. Have each associate explain what items they found, and why they felt they would be a good complimenting purchase, and then add up the total value of this imaginary sale. Then give the associate who has come up with the most profitable list of add-on sales some small recognition—say, five or ten dollars.

This is all about more sales and you want to instill the fact that the more you sell, the more everyone makes. This exercise brings a lot of fun and laughter as you discuss the items and add up their value. Watch how this simple little exercise translates into more added sales during the days that follow. Better yet, use it as a kick-off to a week-long contest on suggestive selling. Give prizes for first, second and third place. Make it competitive—you can also post each day's results in the back room to make it fun for everyone.

It's Not "Pushy"

I have heard store owners complain that some sales people feel that they might be pushing something on the customer that they don't want. My answer to that is always the same: If the customer doesn't want it, she will let you know. If you don't ask, you will never know—and your customer may have missed out on something that she simply hadn't thought of, something that could make her day (or her outfit). One of the main responsibilities of the sales associate is to give the customer the opportunity to make the purchase. After all, isn't that is what sales associates are being paid to do? And who better to make an add-on suggestion than a sales associate, who has product knowledge, a sense of what goes together, and information on what's trendy, fresh and/or unique?

Retailers continually struggle to reinvent themselves, refine assortments and closely manage expenses and inventory. I encourage all retailers to pay more attention to suggestive selling practices this coming year as well. Teach yourself to listen to the techniques retailers outside the footwear industry use in suggestive selling. It doesn't matter whether they're selling tires, food, jewelry, books or something else. **How** they do it could be adaptable to your store, for whatever kinds of additional items you carry. And the next time someone asks you if "you want fries with that?" you'll be able to recognize suggestive selling for what it really is: more sales and better profits.

January/February 2010

Top 10 Secrets for
Success Now

◆

Way back in the 1980s, RMSA put together a document entitled "10 Secrets for Success in Retail Management." I recently rediscovered this publication and thought the message warranted repeating as we enter a new decade. I have taken the liberty of updating the original list a bit for the sake of freshness. What I find most interesting, however, is that the basic principles that make up a successful retail business are pretty much the same now as they were then and always have been.

The main reason why most retail businesses encounter difficulties is that they lack appropriate management techniques. More often than not, money and cash flow issues are the *result* of a problem, not the *cause* of it. Industry analysts have found that there are ten particular management techniques vital to success in retailing. It may be that not all of these areas apply to your operation. Slight improvements in one or two areas alone can sometimes translate into greatly increased profits. With gratitude to RMSA for content and acknowledgment to a certain late-night television host for format, allow me to present the **Top 10 Secrets for Success.**

#10: Expense Management. An annual review of operating expenses once the profit and loss statement is generated at year-end is not sufficient in today's demanding and ever-changing retail climate. Operating expenses need to be planned and budgeted, not left to chance. If we consider that every two percentage points trimmed from current operating expenses could add as much as 60% to net profit, it stands to reason that actual expenses should be compared to planned expenses at least on a quarterly basis.

#9: Markdown Management. It isn't just what sold that counts, but also what hasn't sold. Every slow seller is a drain on earning potential. Excessive markdowns are a result of little or no planning, overbuying or just poor inventory management. Timing of markdowns is key. The longer you wait once you know of a problem, the costlier it will be to remedy.

#8: Visual Merchandise Management. The saying that you seldom get a second chance to make a first impression rings true for this management technique. Visual merchandising is the silent salesperson in any retail operation. Goods well displayed are half sold. We are in a very visual business. It is the presentation of properly displayed merchandise, well planned advertising and good housekeeping that portrays a store's image. First impressions are very important. They influence the customer's conscious and sub-conscious decision making processes. The effective use of color, design, and quality projects the store's attitude and image. I refer to this as a store having "pop" or "wow factor." If accomplished properly, visual merchandising can create customer need and want of an item. If your store lacks the talent to create "pop," hire a visual merchandiser on a contract basis. With the downsizing and reorganizing of retailers due to the economy, a plethora or talent in this area abounds in nearly every region of the country.

#7: Customer Service Management. Customers are the most important people to any retail establishment. They are not dependent on us; we are dependent on them. It is critical for management to develop training programs for employees. Training should be an ongoing program encompassing specific objectives that reinforce employee development and company policy. (And remember that even long-term employees need training—regarding new products, new product technology, fashion trends, communicating effectively with customers, and so on. Nobody is ever so skilled that there is nothing left to learn.)

#6: Customer Analysis Management. Retailers often refer to their "regular" customers without realizing that up to 18% of these customers are probably lost on an annual basis. Customers move, shop other stores, and eventually die. These attrition factors are referred to as the three "Ds"—death, desertion, and dissatisfaction. It is important to review your customer base periodically to see how it has changed. Perhaps you need to change some things to attract new customers. Be open to this. People shop differently today than they did in the past and they will probably shop differently in the future.

#5: Debt Management. The objective here is to keep debt at a minimum and cash flow at a maximum, especially in 2010. Outstanding debt obligations that impede credit may starve an operation of fresh salable inventory which could ultimately affect sales and cash flow.

#4: Sound Profit Management. "What gets measured, gets managed," according to management guru Peter Drucker. With all of the management tools available today thanks to technology, there is absolutely no excuse not to have current data relative to your business immediately accessible. This list of information needed for sound profit management includes, but is not limited to a cash flow statement, balance sheet, income statement, vendor profitability report, fast and slow seller report, and sales and inventory forecast (open-to-buy plan).

#3: Self-Control Management. This technique may be the most significant of all and too often the least applied. Goal-setting is the starting point. Reasonable and attainable goals must be set for all areas of the operation. Successful implementation of all of the techniques discussed here are essential if one's goals are to be achieved. Prioritize your time. All too often, store owners micro-manage the most insignificant portions of their businesses. Tackle the most important tasks first, those being the ones that could have the greatest financial impact on the business.

#2: Inventory Management. This topic is best described in three terms: turnover, cash flow, and gross margin return on investment (GMROI). Of these, turnover is by far the most essential. Seldom have I encountered a retailer experiencing cash flow issues that had a good turnover rate. It should be remembered that for every week of improvement in annual sell-though, cash flow increases by approximately one percent of sales. Nobody comes in your store looking for merchandise that was received last year. Increases in profitable business come from a constant flow of properly timed new merchandise. For maximum sales, focus more on what is selling, rather than on what *isn't*.

#1: Dollar Planning Management. Retailers do not fail from overbuying. They fail when they can't pay for their overbuying. The development of a sound merchandise planning and open-to-buy program is crucial to the survival of any retail operation. Forecasting and planning must be based on the sound evaluation of current and projected sales and inventory figures. Classification merchandising or the development of trends by type and end-use of merchandise is essential. Buying merchandise in the right amounts, timing deliveries properly, and having the proper selection of styles with adequate assortment planning are the keys to increased profits.

_____

March/April 2010

Pet Peeves: Things Retailers
Do That Really Bug Me!

◆

Anyone who has been around the retail game for any length of time probably has subconsciously compiled a list of minor annoyances that drive them bonkers. These would consist of the little, common sense things that you notice in stores and ask yourself, "Why would someone do that?" Here is my list of things that some retailers do that, well, simply bug me. Maybe they bug you too?

Where ever I go, I notice store windows. Have you ever visited a town and noticed a store that feels they need to cram a sample of everything they carry in the front window in order to get their message out? This drives me out of my mind. The confusion and clutter created by doing this actually have the opposite effect on shoppers. They don't get any message at all. When it comes to store windows and in-store displays, keeping things simple is always a better way to go.

Call Attention to THAT?

Sometimes the natural tendency for retailers attempting to move merchandise that no one wants to buy is to actually give it *more* attention. They do this by putting the slow-moving goods in the window, creating a display in the store or—worse yet—spending advertising money to promote a "dog." This is a failed strategy void of all common sense. Sure, we need to rid our stocks of problem merchandise as quickly as possible, but we don't need to show the world our problems by highlighting trouble merchandise. You can't grow volume by constantly focusing on what no one wants to buy. Volume is built when stores feature what customers want now!

What would happen if you built a house without an architect first drawing up a blueprint? Unless you were very lucky, the result would likely be disastrous. Yet this is exactly the gamble that retailers take when they buy without a well-constructed merchandise plan. Unless the retail guardian angel intervenes, more often than not, stocks will be out of balance, leading to stifled sales and missed buying opportunities. Overbuying is also likely to occur. As a result, poor cash flow, high markdowns and slower turnover will prevail.

Have you ever known of a store owner (or buyer) that buys a little bit from every vendor that calls on him or her? These are people who have a hard time saying **"NO."** They don't want to hurt anyone's feelings, especially since the rep came all the way to the store "just to show me the line." Well, that's his job. Yours is to buy a well-balanced assortment that has meaning to your customers. When you buy a little from everyone, you end up with a whole lot of nothing. This practice leads to overbuying, duplication, and confusion to the customer. In addition, the lines are not meaningful to the store and conversely, the store is not important to the manufacturer.

Don't Hover, Do Be Knowledgeable

I hate going into a store prepared to buy, only to be ignored. It actually makes me mad. I don't need to be hovered over, but I do expect to be greeted cheerfully when I walk in and have a knowledgeable salesperson available to answer any questions I may have. While I know we are all busy, I believe that's not too much to ask.

I like to be sold. I understand the sales process and I appreciate other sales professionals that do too. It matters not to me if I am buying a pair of socks or a new car. I want to be sold! Don't just read the label to me when I am asking a product-related question, tell me something I don't know. Providing extra information adds value to my shopping experience and makes me feel better about my purchase.

It drives me nuts to go into a store and see a four-way display fixture jammed with three times more merchandise than it was ever intended to hold. Typically, the same display will also be holding multiple lines, styles and even colors that don't go together. This merchandising technique usually is associated with an "overbuyer," or at the very least an individual who does not understand how vital a component visual merchandising is to increased sales.

How's Your Presentation?

When I see empty racks, shelves or other fixtures lacking inventory, I could just scream. With expenses and competition being what they are today, it is so important that retailers scrutinize their merchandise presentation at all times in order to maximize sales.

Cluttered and hard-to-read print ads are simply a waste of advertising dollars. They too drive me crazy.

I equate a dirty store with a lazy owner. Floors should be mopped or vacuumed daily. Racks should be dusted—and don't forget the tops of the glass cubes. They are huge dust gatherers.

Hand-printed display signs are the absolute worst. I don't care if your printing is exceptional. A professionally printed sign says a lot about your image.

When I go into a store with ridiculous pricing, the veins in my neck bulge. This is the store where the owner didn't set the retail price and told the marking room to take a certain percentage markup. In this store, you will find prices like $42.37 next to something marked $36.84. What's that all about? You will find a similar approach to pricing at this store when the sale price is literally 1/3 off the original price. I am talking 33.333% off. $36.84 now becomes, you got it...$24.68. Simply ridiculous!

These are just some items that have been bothering me for a while. I feel much better sharing them with you. If I missed anything that bugs you, shoot me a quick email so that I can update my list.

_____

May/June 2010

Is Your Store
Out of Balance?

◆

My suspicion is that few folks reading this article seldom, if ever, ponder this issue. Given that all merchants today are searching for alternative methods to grow top line revenue, inventory balance should not be overlooked.

Over the past few years, retailers have taken the scalpel to all but the most essential expenses, labored over methods to improve inventory turnover, scoured markets in search of new and unique products and relentlessly hounded vendors for promotional goods to boost margins. Merchants are quick to complain about late deliveries, product quality, unmotivated sales people, even weather conditions, yet I can't recall a store wondering about the one thing they can readily control: the **balance of the inventory** in their stores.

Harmony & Proportion

Of the several definitions found for the word "balance," the meaning that I find to be most apt is "to bring into harmony or proportion." Nothing functions at its best when out of balance. When the steering wheel on your car vibrates at a certain speed, most likely your wheels are out of balance. Not addressing the issue results in an uncomfortable ride not to mention unnecessary tire wear which ultimately will cost you more money. Golfers are reminded to stay "in balance" if they are to derive the maximum result from each swing. If you work too much, play too hard, drink or eat too much, have too much stress or do pretty much anything else to excess, your life can become out of balance as well. The consequences of an out of balance life run the gambit from possible physical and emotional issues to relationship and financial problems.

Balance is also important for a retail store. It is impossible for sales volume to be maximized unless all classifications have the correct levels of inventory, the ideal mix of styles, a well thought out combination of vendors and a selection of price points from which the customer may choose.

Symptoms versus Causes

One of the more readily apparent symptoms of a store out of balance is the lack of overall sales growth. The causes of the imbalance take some additional detective work to unveil. Oftentimes, an out of balance operation can be disguised by financials that appear to be fine on the surface. A few months ago, I spoke with a store owner whose overall merchandising statistics looked fairly healthy. Store turnover was at or slightly above industry norms, initial and maintained markup numbers were acceptable and operating expenses appeared to be spot on. The retailer's concern was that for the third consecutive year volume had not grown; in fact, it had slipped a few percentage points. I offered to review the classification sales data for the preceding year and within minutes the problem became obvious. Two of the store's largest contributing classifications were turning much faster than the highest industry benchmarks. Sales in these classifications were outperforming the first of month retail inventory levels and potential sales were being missed.

The store was literally starving these important classes. You might be thinking that this should be obvious. The reason that it is **not** is due to the fact that most retailers are consumed with primarily looking at sales figures—and any increase is a good increase, no matter how it comes. Four other categories were turning substantially slower than they should have been, thus tying up dollars that could be spent supporting the growth classes.

Monitor Activity Regularly

A plan was put in place to regularly monitor the sales activity and place reorders in a timely manner. In the classes that were not performing up to par, the oldest merchandise became the target of the most aggressive markdowns, followed by broken sizes, discontinued styles and colors, and vendors that the store had elected not to move forward with.

Underperforming lines were also eliminated from the assortment plan and the store's merchants worked diligently to avoid duplications in future buying. What followed shortly thereafter was, not surprisingly, a very healthy increase in sales volume.

Since most retailers are often too close to the situation to see the best solution, it is usually a good practice to have a trained outsider review your class data and make recommendations. Rarely is there a situation where bringing the harmony and proportion back to the inventory does not lead to increased sales and better cash flow.

_____

July/August 2010

An Incentive Plan
That Really Works

◆

Nearly every retailer that I have worked with has asked me at some point if I can help them develop an effective incentive structure that is also simple to manage. The answer is yes, but there are some basic rules that must be followed for a bonus plan to work.

Begin by deciding what you are trying to accomplish. Are you creating a program for the sales staff, the buying department, or the management personnel? A one-size-fits-all approach may not work for all three. In some stores, these positions may even be combined. For the purpose of this discussion, let's focus on a buyer/manager scenario. We will assume that the buyer in this case is responsible for the department's sales, assortment and quantity of products being offered, maintained margin and shrinkage.

Be Clear and Realistic

When introducing any incentive plan, it is important to make certain that the rules are attainable and measurable, and simple to understand. A plan that is too complex or loaded with caveats and disclaimers soon takes on an almost "gotcha" like feeling. Keep it simple and straightforward. Remember, the goal is to reward an employee who has achieved his or her corporate goals. Programs laden with loopholes or "outs" for the employer only serve to reduce morale and are therefore counter-productive. Make sure the goals set are realistic. Sure, you want to challenge employees and help them grow business, but creating an unattainable target may in fact cause the employee to dismiss the plan altogether. Benchmark numbers must be objective, not subjective; they must also be measurable. A point of sale system or merchandise planning program that captures this data may be credible sources from which to derive needed data.

I once developed a program for a store that had a rather significant pay-out if everyone achieved their preset goals. When the program was first proposed, however, the owner explained that there was no way such a rich payout would ever get his support. "We've never done anything like this before," he said. "What if we can't pay the bonuses?"

Built-in Safeguards

What finally won his approval was the fact that the program had built-in safeguards. If objectives were not attained, bonuses would not be paid. If, on the other hand, all initiatives were met, the increase in sales and profitability would offset the generous payout several times over. He soon discovered that his employees became more motivated and more enthusiastic about their jobs. They actually became engaged in the process, which was the ultimate reward. They seemed to embrace the structure the plan provided, as well as the potential of monetary gain.

I prefer a four-part program because it satisfies all required objectives and is a win-win situation for the store and the employee. The four parts of the program are as follows: **sales, maintained markup, turnover, and shrinkage.** Each component is worth a certain dollar value. The dollar amount is arbitrary, but needs to be something substantial. I will use the figure of $1,000 to illustrate how this works. The owner and the employee arrive at a sales goal for the upcoming year that fits into the company's overall growth plans. Previous sales history will be helpful is establishing these goals. A maintained markup goal is then agreed upon, followed by a turnover objective for the classification, department or store. A shrinkage percentage is the final piece of the puzzle. At the end of the year, bonus money is awarded for all met objectives. If an employee achieves all four objectives, he/she would then receive $4,000. If only two objectives are attained, then only $2,000 will be paid out.

Variations

I have experimented with variations of this premise that work well. One idea is to use GMROI as a substitute for either the turn or margin objectives if it works in the employee's favor. This gives the plan added flexibility, as the employee can substitute the achieved GMROI goal if either the turnover or margin goals have been missed. Another option is an additional bonus which I refer to as a "kicker." If all four objectives are met an additional $1,000 "kicker" is paid, bringing the total bonus payout to $5,000. If three out of the four points are met, the "kicker" is $500. If fewer than three goals are met, there is no additional bonus money available. The "kicker" encourages focus on all facets of the plan.

Checks and Balances

A common mistake on incentive plans is to pay on sales only. This can be disastrous if the sales are generated through markdowns or aggressive discounting. If the store pays on gross margin or maintained markup only, there is no incentive to improve turnover and therefore cash flow. If turnover is the only consideration, the objective might be reached at the expense of margin. A combination of sales volume, margin improvement and turnover protects the store, thus insuring profitability, while providing incentive to the employee.

Review in Private, Pay in Public

Always conduct the review when you say that you will. Employees expect this and count on it. Review should be conducted privately and should not be put off. Areas in need of improvement should be addressed at this time. For future reference, it is a good business practice to keep signed and dated copies of each review within an employees personnel file.

Remember the saying your mother taught you about it being better to give than to receive? You now get the best of both worlds. The fact that you are paying bonuses at all indicates some level of success. Too many stores miss the opportunity to celebrate employee achievements. Make the payout a celebration. What better way to instill morale than to recognize an employee in front of his or her peers for a job well done? Perhaps a staff meeting, or even a rewards dinner including significant others, might be in order. The ultimate goal should be to pay out maximum bonuses to all eligible parties. If you are able to do this, you will not only be rewarding the employees that helped you achieve the corporate goals, you will be setting the stage for even greater results in the future through the motivation, recognition, and job enrichment that a well-managed incentive program offers.

September/October 2010

The Seven Deadly
Retail Sins

---------------- ◆ ----------------

The Seven Deadly Sins, first identified by St. John Cassian and later re-fined by Pope St. Gregory the Great, have been with us for more than 1500 years. As Cassian put it, "They provide us keys to understanding our faults and the actions that result, and a framework for self knowledge."

The original Seven Deadly Sins were Pride, Greed, Envy, Lust, Sloth, Anger, and Gluttony.

While I would relish the challenge of drawing parallels between the original list and shortcomings evident with some modern day retailers, I will resist the temptation to do so. What I will offer instead is:

My list of Seven Deadly Retail Sins, along with their corresponding virtues. You may find yourself guilty of one or two—or perhaps several. That being the case, one can rest easy in the knowledge that along with repentance comes total redemption. Hopefully, this list will prompt you to come up with your own personal list of retail maladies, which is the ultimate goal.

My Seven Deadly Retail Sins are Overbuying, Underbuying, Not Attending Markets, No Markdown Strategy, Not Controlling Operating Expenses, Under-Utilization of Technology and Poor Planning.

Let's consider these individually.

Overbuying

This one should be obvious. The consequences of this "sin" include reduced margins due to high markdowns, cluttered stores, confusing assortments, stocks that are out of balance, slow turnover, poor cash flow, and increased expenses.

Virtue: Following your open-to-buy plan.

Underbuying

Perhaps not as obvious, but a "sin" nonetheless. When underbuying occurs, sales opportunities are missed. This problem is generally caused by lack of proper merchandise planning at the classification level. Examples of underbuying range from not responding to needed reorders to not buying narrow and deep enough to positively impact sales volume.

Virtue: A bottom-up sales and inventory forecast at the class and store level.

Not Attending Markets

Not attending markets or trade shows on a regular basis is a retail "sin." This is the perfect opportunity to keep your store fresh and one step ahead of the competition. New lines can be discovered, orders already written but not yet shipped can be reviewed, educational seminars can be attended, vendor relations can be nurtured, and major retailers in the area can be shopped.

Virtue: Attend trade shows and markets two to four times a year, depending on industry segment.

No Markdown Strategy

Markdowns in and of themselves are not a problem. Markdowns taken at the wrong time, in the wrong amount and for the wrong reasons are a **big** problem. Excessive markdowns taken at season end can be very costly if the classification was overbought to begin with. Proper monitoring of sales and inventory during the season can help prevent costly markdowns at season end. Remember, "The first markdown is the cheapest"—so make it count.

Virtue: Have a well developed markdown strategy for your store.

Not Controlling Operating Expenses

If you pay too much for rent, chances are the only ones making money will be the landlord and the vendors! Review your lease(s) annually to make sure you are paying market or, preferably, below. Most retailers only look at their lease when it comes up for renewal. This can be a costly mistake, especially in today's business climate. I strongly recommend hiring the services of a good lease negotiator to act on your behalf unless you are personally very skilled in this area. They can usually save their fees several times over, and you will know you are not leaving money on the table. Review payroll and other expenses annually and compare to industry benchmarks.

Virtue: Develop an operating expense budget and review at least annually.

Under-Utilization of Technology

There was a time not so long ago when only a handful of cutting-edge merchants embraced the latest technology of the day. Today, not understanding and using technology puts a retailer in jeopardy of being left behind. Point-of-sale (POS) systems not only track sales and inventory, but can also help manage work schedules and analyze buying habits. Social media outlets help today's merchants get their message out quickly and cost effectively. Store web sites provide store information and can serve as a vehicle for additional sales, especially when linked to a vendor's site. Good POS systems are a major investment. All too often, the investment in them is under-utilized, resulting only in bar-coded tickets and electronic cash drawers.

Virtue: Take the time to understand and maximize all forms of technology available to you.

Poor Planning

Poor planning is almost as dangerous as no planning at all. From a forecasting perspective, poor planning can be to blame for many of the "sins" described above. From an accounting perspective, poor planning can lead to poor cash management—and cash management is the lifeblood of most retail operations.

Virtue: Spend time developing, implementing and revising all planning aspects in your company.

Just as no human is perfect, no retailer is without occasional "sin." Confession of these and other infractions, as well as implementation of the virtues described above, will certainly help put you on the pathway to eternal salvation and secure your place in retail heaven.

Go forth, my retail brothers and sisters, and "sin" no more!

November/December 2010

The Truth
About Markdowns

◆

The word itself strikes fear in the hearts of most retailers. Call it by whatever term you wish—price adjustment, promotion, or just plain sale, the translation is the same and conjures up all sorts of negative emotions. The fact remains, however, that any reduction in the retail price is really a **markdown**.

Most folks in the retail business have an inherent disdain for the very word. Taking too many markdowns represents failure in some area or another. Overbuying, duplication, poor timing of deliveries, bad assortment planning, are all recognized causes of markdowns. Excessive markdowns raise the cost of goods sold and result in a reduction in gross margin. When margin levels fall below those of operating expenses, the store has a net loss.

To more fully understand this retail nemesis, let's uncover some truths about markdowns.

Truth #1: Markdowns are the tuition retailers must pay for the education they receive from their customers. A lot can be learned about how to buy and price merchandise from past mistakes. If you really want to know where you screwed up, carefully survey your markdown rack.

Truth #2: Since markdowns are a way of life as well as an important part of the retail business, it is important that a markdown plan be established. Base the markdown plan around the turnover goals of the company. For example, if your turnover goal is 3 times, it is important to make sure that stock is sold within a seventeen-week period.

Truth #3: Always explain the markdown to your customer. If you fail to inform your customer that the markdown is for a special buy, end-of-season clearance, weekend-only promotion, or other reason, you risk customers not believing your prices and every sale turning into a mini-auction.

Truth #4: Overbuying is the Number One cause of excessive markdowns. Stores don't go out of business due to high markdowns. They go out of business because they can't pay for their overbuying. If your turnover goal is 3 times, you should be careful not to buy more than you can sell within a four-month time frame.

If you buy more than you can sell, you are predestined to experience either excessive markdowns and reduced margins, or slow turnover and poor cash flow. Faced with this option, it is always better to take the markdowns, clear the inventory and generate cash. I have never seen a store go out of business because turnover was too fast and cash flow was too strong…never! On the contrary, I have seen several stores go under with healthy gross margins on their profit and loss statements.

Truth #5: Most retailers have heard of and would agree with the axiom that the first markdown is the cheapest. What this really refers to is that the first price reduction is an effective one. A "cheap" markdown does not refer to a low percentage reduction that does not significantly generate increased sales. A markdown of 30% that moves merchandise is therefore "cheaper" than a 20% markdown that does not produce the desired results.

Truth #6: The price you paid has nothing to do with the markdown price. The customer does not care what you paid for the product, nor should you. When you get to this point in the sales cycle, your only concern is how quickly you can convert the inventory to cash. From time to time, I encounter stores that are reluctant, and in some cases even refuse, to mark anything below cost. I have never been able to understand the logic behind this thinking. I suppose the mindset is that money is being lost when in reality much more lost revenue is at stake by not getting cash out of slow-selling stock and replacing it with new product. Worse yet is packing goods away in the back room and dragging them out again next year. Your cost is not relevant in a markdown pricing decision.

Truth #7: In most cases, it is a good practice to keep markdown merchandise at the back of the store. You want your customers exposed to new full-price products at every opportunity. Exceptions to this would be store-wide sale events or seasonal clearance time, when a large majority of items are on sale.

Truth #8: Nurture your good customers who do not shop you on price alone. This is where added value comes into play. The cosmetics industry does a great job of this by offering gift-with-purchase items. Thank-you notes to good customers also go a long way in showing a customer that you value their patronage.

Understanding these truths and employing sound markdown management should help turn what to some is a negative part of the business into a positive.

_____

January/February 2011

First, Talk to Your Banker—
and Then?

◆

Most retailers experienced their best holiday season in 2010 since the start of the recession. Despite Christmas falling on a Saturday, and extreme winter weather in some parts of the country hindering sales the last week of December, there was reason a plenty to celebrate the coming of the New Year.

During this past holiday season, I spent some time talking with bankers as well as retailers to find out why banks have been reluctant to extend credit to even the most creditworthy retailers. Until the fall of 2008, obtaining or extending a line of credit with a bank or even getting a small business loan was a relatively painless process. Even as we enter 2011, the banking environment continues to pose challenges for retailers looking for financial assistance.

The Retailer's Perspective

One retailer told me he "hasn't felt much like a customer lately," when describing his long term banking relationship. I also heard from retailers who have had their credit lines reduced by as much as 30% even if the lines weren't currently being used. In yet another instance, a bank wanted seven-figure life insurance policies on both the owner and his wife in order to secure financing for a particular project. One store owner I spoke with shared with me that his bank wasn't even interested in his inventory as collateral, and would only take real estate. Perhaps the most disturbing case involved a bank demanding more collateral from a retailer or risk having the note "called." In the eyes of this bank, more collateral meant *more* inventory, since inventory to the bank is an asset. This was a slow-turning store which keeps inventory levels way above what I would consider optimum. They also resisted taking markdowns on old goods for fear the bank would get nervous when lower gross margin figures were discovered. The store felt they were actually being forced by the bank into making bad business decisions. Talk about being in a no-win situation....

The Bank's Perspective

Even though there have been recent indications that banks are becoming somewhat more willing to lend to small businesses due to a gain in economic momentum, a retailer should expect more reluctance than in previous years. The reasons are several, but mainly come from increased requirements of bank examiners, declines in financial strength in some institutions, a rise in past due and troubled assets, erosion of consumer confidence, and an uncertain outlook for the future.

What You Can Do Now

If you have intentions of ending up with more than a cup of complimentary coffee and a free logo pen from the next visit to your local banker, consider the following suggestions:

- Communicate effectively and often. Bankers don't like surprises.

- Provide the banker with the information requested in a timely fashion. There are reasons behind every request.

- Bankers look for positive trends. If you can deliver good news, do so.

- Bankers are constantly looking to show management and examiners areas that will reduce the level of risk to the bank going forward. If you have a line of credit that can be reduced due to lack of use, consider reducing it.

- Bankers are working harder because of increased scrutiny across many levels. Be prepared to supply more frequent financial data.

- Don't be combative or adversarial. Banking is a relationship business. Work with your banker, not against him.

- Strive to become the "A" customer, even though you may not always feel like one. This doesn't mean that you have to have the best balance sheet or the highest volume store. Being responsive, truthful, timely, reasonable, available, and cooperative will go a long way toward strengthening your banking relationships.

Continued uncertainty will most likely challenge retailers throughout 2011. To cope with an ever-changing economic and financial climate, there are steps you can take now. To begin, negotiate the longest payment plan you can with vendors. Try to sell at least half of what you are buying before you have to pay the invoice and buy what you can from vendors who offer you the best terms.

Consider the merits of the following strategy. Assume for a moment, that you are able to negotiate 60-day terms with a few key vendors and that you turn your inventory three times.

Work the Numbers

3 turns = 121.6 days of supply (365 divided by 3)

Approximately half of the merchandise is sold by the time the invoice is due.

Would it ever be possible to sell all of the merchandise prior to paying for it? If you can get 90-day terms and turn the inventory four times, for all practical purposes, the entire inventory will be sold by the time the invoice is payable.

4 turns = 91 days of supply (365 divided by 4)

Simple math will show that 2 turns = 26 weeks of supply (WOS), 2.5 turns = 20.8 WOS, and 3 turns = 17.3 WOS. An improvement of only one week in annual sell-through increases cash flow by approximately 1% of annual sales. This point alone makes the case for all retailers to strive for increased turnover.

Use of personal credit cards is also becoming a very common practice when paying for merchandise. I know of a retailer who prefers to use a credit card when possible. This practice not only provides for longer payment options, "but an additional **big** benefit is hundreds and hundreds of dollars of free airfare," as one retailer told me. This merchant also takes advantage of the points he gets to obtain gift cards which are used as employee rewards.

Just because credit is more difficult to come by now than it was in the past need not suggest that today's retailer abandon all hope and adopt a "management by crisis" mentality. It does, however, mean that creative ways to finance growth be considered—and improving inventory turnover should be the Number 1 way.

March/April 2011

How To Drive
Sales Profitably

◆

There is an old retail saying that goes something like this: "Increased sales volume cures all ills." All retailers seem to breathe a little easier when sales are rising. Invoices are easier to pay, expenses aren't a problem, credit lines are reduced or paid off, and cash flow isn't a concern. Positive sales growth is a retailer's validation that he or she is doing a good job and is in control of the business. In other words, it's **fun** to go to work!

Top line revenue growth is the most vital component of a thriving retail business. A store can have great margins, phenomenal stock turnover and an outstanding gross margin return on investment (GMROI), but if sales aren't sufficient to cover normal operating expenses, you've got a problem.

Review Financials First

When a store comes to me with this problem, one of the first things I do is review the financial statements. It is important to get a baseline on the business. The profit and loss statement (P/L) helps ascertain that the cost of goods sold is within industry norms, and that operating expenses are reasonable and typical for the type and location of the store in question.

The first portion of the P/L provides information relative to sales volume and the profitability of those sales. Look for a percentage change from one year to the next if available. The gross margin number shows how effective the operation is at selling merchandise at full price. A GM% that is too low would be an indication of excessive markdowns and/or an inadequate initial mark-up.

When evaluating operating expenses, primarily focus on occupancy and payroll costs, as those tend to consume the largest portion of the budget. Since the discussion is on sales growth, or in this case, the lack thereof, a review of the sales and promotion expense is also in order.

With regard to the balance sheet, look for three main things:

1. How much money does the store have available now?

2. How much money does the store owe?

3. Are there loan obligations that need to be met and if so how much?

Calculate Breakeven

Assuming that no major issues are discovered in the review process, the next step is to determine the store's breakeven point. This is the sales number that must be attained for the operation to be viable. There are two ways to get this number, the long, complicated way (probably your accountant's way) and the quick, simple way (my way). Let's go with my way. To get a quick and accurate breakeven figure take your total annual operating expenses divided by the anticipated gross margin percentage.

Formula: total expenses/anticipated GM%

Example: $440,000/47%=$936,170

Why Aren't Sales Growing?

If the financial statements are in reasonable shape, the next determination to make is why sales aren't growing. There are several factors that can come in to play, including location, overall economy, dollars per square foot, advertising and promotional activity including social media marketing, attitude and ability of sales associates, ownership and management involvement, assortment, pricing, and most importantly, the **freshness of the merchandise.**

Let's focus on inventory freshness. I will restate a question posed previously: what sells faster, merchandise from past seasons or last year that you have carried over, or fresh new products that have just arrived in time for the new season? Admittedly this seems to be a ridiculous question, at least on the surface. That said, I am amazed as to why so many retailers fall into the trap of not adequately clearing out seasonal goods. We are not dealing with wine or antiques here—this stuff doesn't get any better with age. It just costs the business more money the longer it sits unsold on the store's shelves (or, worse yet, in a box in the back room).

I recently worked with a women's and children's shoe retailer who was doing this very thing. Business seemed reasonably fine on the surface, but invoice payments were always running behind, discounts were being missed, and cash flow was usually tight. When reviewing the age of the merchandise by classification, a very revealing discovery came to light: In three significant categories, merchandise was very slow in turning. In fact the old 80/20 rule was in play with 80% of the sales coming from about 20% of the inventory—and it wasn't the old stuff that was selling. Surprise, surprise!

Fresh Inventory = More Sales

After a heart-to-heart discussion with the owner, it was decided that anything over six months old would be liquidated as soon as possible. The initial misgivings that I heard regarding impact on margins soon dissipated when the back room was cleared out of all old goods, the sale room was empty, past due invoices were paid, and money was in the bank instead of being tied up in product that in some cases had had not one, but two birthdays. Another important side benefit was that this owner went to market with expanded open-to-buy dollars in these categories for fresh new inventory.

The end result is that overall inventory has been reduced significantly, sales volume is stronger because the store has fresher merchandise, and gross margin is healthier because now more product is being sold at full price.

The moral of the story is that fresh inventory in the right quantity and the right classifications drives sales volume.

May/June 2011

Twelve Questions Determine
Your Readiness

◆

As a retailer, you generally enter every month with two very different sets of emotions, excitement and fear. The excitement comes from hope that the month could be terrific, the fear is that the rest of the year could be a financial failure. You carefully watch the evening news, read the financial section of the daily newspaper, and vigilantly review trade papers, all with the hope that you will get the answer to the question, *Will my business be successful or not?*

The reality is, no matter what the analysts, newspapers, or networks predict, your company generally never reflects their predictions. Ponder this question: If the industry you are in predicted a three percent gain, would you do anything differently than if the forecasters had projected a twelve percent gain or a six percent decrease? Doubtful! If sales were trending up five percent, would you cut back if the news reports indicated otherwise? Probably not. Are you going to adjust your on-order or inventory because of the country's financial problems? Have you trimmed your inventory because the market has been inconsistent?

Let's face it: The success or failure of your company is in your hands. If you are prepared, I mean *really* ready to do business, chances are what the analysts say won't matter. The key is being honest with yourself. Are you prepared and determined? Take this simple test to find out. Ask yourself these "Twelve Questions for Retailers" to determine your level of readiness:

1. Have you done anything really different in preparing your store than you did last year?

2. Have you had a good year so far?

3. Have you invested more time or energy training your sales staff, versus last year?

4. Does your store look cleaner and fresher than last year?

5. Is your merchandise more appealing than last year? Be truthful.

6. Have you added fresh lines to your mix?

7. Are you advertising more than last year?

8. Are you really in touch with your customers?

9. Can you name three things your company has done in the last few months to separate itself from its competitors?

10. How many times have customers commented on how good your store looks in the past thirty days?

11. Have you established a goal and are you following the plan?

12. Do you have special events planned?

Scoring

If your honest answer is "yes" to **eight or more** questions, forget what the experts say—you're on your way.

If you answered "yes" on **at least five** questions, you should have a very good year-end.

If you answered "yes" on **three or four** questions, you'll probably have a better than average year.

If you answered "yes" to **less than three**, pull out the newspaper, sit back, and hope for the best.

If you answered "no" to all twelve, you might want to consider another line of work.

Executing properly, buying correctly, keeping inventory fresh, controlling markdowns, landing new lines, attracting new customers, and keeping sales associates motivated and trained, will position your company so that it is always prepared to grow.

Why is it so important to be prepared? Why must you work so hard and smart to succeed? Because competition continues to change and today's savvy customers show much more discretion in their buying habits. The degree of success you achieve will be determined by the level of your commitment to operate the business in a more effective and efficient fashion.

Retailers must constantly strive to distinguish their identity by maintaining creativity. Being different than the competition has always been important. Today, it's mandatory.

––––––––––

July/August 2011

What's Your Excuse?

◆

"The weather is killing business."

"The economy is keeping people from buying."

"My competitors are copying my lines and breaking price too soon."

"High gas prices are keeping customers from traveling."

"My sales people aren't working hard enough."

"We have always done it this way in the past."

Blah, blah, blah....

Excuses seem to be a part of some retailers' genetic makeup. We've all heard excuses, and perhaps even used a few of them ourselves. We use excuses to divert blame to an uncontrollable circumstance or element. Blaming the weather or the economy when business is not good is much more convenient—and internally palatable—than more introspective approaches of problem solving.

By one definition, an excuse is an expression of regret for failure to do something. In other words, it is a justification or a reason why something did not happen. It was recently suggested to me that what I have chosen to label as excuses might actually be business problems. I will concede that point: Bad weather certainly can hinder sales. And yes, difficult economic times will make some customers pull back.

In light of these "business problems," the question that needs to be asked is: Why do I see so many stores doing so incredibly well? Recognizing the difference between a true business problem and a lame excuse can go a long way toward improving not only the way you approach your business, but perhaps your outlook on life in general.

I recently asked my clients this question and one of the responses is enclosed nearly verbatim. (Honesty compels me to admit that I took out the names; my editor took out some words generally considered a bit vulgar in print.) This retailer said it better than I ever could.

Dear Ritchie,

Good question! I too have heard (and used) weather and economic issues as my number one and two excuses. However, my weekly chats with [another retailer] made me realize that we're both experiencing the same weather and economic conditions and yet her store was rockin'! I needed to stop being a "Candy-_ _ _" retailer and relying on lame excuses. (You may use this verbatim if you wish!)

Our weather has [been awful] and yet I still had a "Kick-_ _ _" Month! In other words, I have great solutions, not excuses!

- *On the RMSA front, I kept track of my best selling subclasses and filled in throughout the month in those areas.*

- *On the customer communication front, I made a conscious effort to get out no more than one e-mail per week. Every other week, I ran promotional specials for my Facebook fans.*

- *I took advantage of the Mother's Day Holiday and sent out a postcard mailing to all of my customers.*

- *I printed a "Best Customer" list and had my employees call and invite them in to see our new Spring Merchandise.*

- *Last but not least, I printed a "New Customer" list and my employees and I have been writing hand-written Thank You Notes to all of our new customers including a $25.00 Gift Certificate in appreciation for them shopping at my store!*

Above all, I am a very present store owner! For the most part, I am in my store at least six days a week! When I hear people grumbling I can't help but think that they're just too lazy to do the work.

Hope this helps!

P.S. — Latest excuse from a fellow retailer—not enough foot traffic! (aka—candy-_ _ _ retailer!)

Wow! You know what my editor took out, though I am sure we have all heard far worse, but there is no missing the point. Quit complaining and pointing fingers. Simply put, **no more excuses**. Take a moment to step back and take a long look in the mirror at what **you** can do to change your own business problems. Your approach may differ from the one above, but the point is to train your thought process to focus on the positive and see just how quickly things begin to change for the better.

September/October 2011

Turn, Turn, Turn

———————— ◆ ————————

One of the classic musical pieces of the 1960s was a song called "Turn, Turn, Turn." Put to music originally by Pete Seeger, and later recorded by The Byrds among others, the song is adapted almost entirely from the Book of Ecclesiastes in the Bible's Old Testament. The basic premise of the song is that there is a time and place for all things. Being consumed by retail when I was growing up, I was certain that someone had written a #1 hit about turnover. What did I know?

"Turn, Turn, Turn" should be every retailer's theme song today. If we put a retail spin on the lyrics, **increasing sales volume** would undoubtedly be the opening verse. Following would be a refrain on selling inventory more quickly. In other words, **faster turn!** Notice I did not mention margin. The margin that you maintain is irrelevant if sales are not sufficient to cover expenses and merchandise receipts.

I currently work with shoe retailers who are achieving turnover rates of more than three times annually, and feel that four is within reach. These are stores in the size and width business just like yours, that are not missing sales, enjoy good margins, and are growing sales volume. They get it.

Increased turn and sales growth can be achieved by adhering to the following protocol:

- Readily identify hot selling styles and trends, and react accordingly.

- Work with resources that can supply product.

- Negotiate stock balancing agreements in advance for poor performing styles.

- Minimize seasonal carryover and avoid packing goods away for the next big sale.

- Reserve Open-To-Buy (OTB) for off-price opportunities that can be volume drivers.

- Pay close attention to scheduling deliveries, so that there is a constant flow of fresh merchandise arriving regularly. Employ this keep-it-fresh merchandising philosophy, as opposed to front-loading at the beginning of each season in hopes that you planned (guessed) correctly about future business.

- Chase product when possible. This is a much preferred strategy to over-buying and trying to cancel. Any manufacturer's rep will support me on this.

- Don't become the vendor's warehouse.

- Negotiate longer terms. Even an extra 30-60 days will help cash flow and give you an opportunity to sell some of the product prior to the invoice coming due.

I have taken the liberty of rewriting some of King Solomon's original words, but the tune remains the same. I invite all of you to sing along with me. Here we go…

To every class Turn, Turn, Turn, there is a season Turn, Turn, Turn, and a time for every markdown under heaven.

A time to buy, a time to sell; A time to reorder, a time to review;

A time to plan, a time to promote; A time to markup, a time to markdown the old stuff that isn't selling.

A time to open, a time to close; A time to hire, a time to train; A time to motivate, a time to unload sales people whose selling costs continually exceed10%.

A time to relocate, a time to remodel; A time to lease, a time to renegotiate your lease especially if it's over 8-10% of your sales.

A time to transfer, a time to cancel; A time to test new vendors, a time to drop lines that no longer work or are not profitable .

A time to forecast deliveries, A time to budget expenses; A time for a new POS system, A time for Facebook, Twitter, and perhaps even Groupon; A time to build your OTB plan by classification and store from the bottom up.

I readily admit that my version may not end up being the #1 hit that The Byrds had. I also added some lines so that folks on the operations side wouldn't feel left out. The central theme however is that improving turnover IS the pathway to profitability. Faster turning stores have better cash flow, larger sales increases, and way better GMROI.

I swear it's not too late!

November/December 2011

New Year's Resolutions

◆

Why do we go through the charade of making idle promises to ourselves each year, promises that are usually dismissed or forgotten by the time the effects of New Year's Eve have worn off? Have you ever noticed all the new faces in the health clubs in January, people sporting the cross trainers and workout wear acquired over the Holidays? The "newness" is so obvious it is almost comical, and most will have abandoned their physical aspirations come spring. New Year's resolutions also remind me in many ways of politicians who make grandiose promises in hopes of electoral victory, rarely following through on any of them.

Still, making resolutions for the upcoming year is a time-honored tradition with roots tracing back to Babylonian times. In 153 B.C, Janus—the mythical king of early Rome—gave his name to the first month of the calendar. Janus was always depicted with two faces, one looking back on past events, the other forward to the future. The early Christians believed the first day of the year should be spent reflecting on past mistakes and resolving to improve oneself in the coming year. Today, many people look at the New Year as a chance to start over, to rid themselves of bad habits and take on a fresh, positive way of life. Hence, history gives us the modern day New Year's resolution which generally encompasses everything from self improvement, to improved finances, to better health.

As you reflect on the past year and look forward to the next professionally, take time to recognize past accomplishments that had a positive impact on your business. As you consider areas you would like to improve on for the upcoming year, focus on goals, objectives and initiatives that are attainable and realistic.

I want to avoid offering up a smorgasbord of suggestions that would most likely be forgotten as quickly as last season's markdowns. However, here is one resolution that every merchant should make each and every year:

Resolve to: Sell more merchandise more quickly!

That's it. Resolution-making, at least from a business standpoint, is over. Here's why. Selling more of your inventory more quickly achieves a multitude of favorable results. First, we have resolved to have a sales increase. This increase will be driven not by profit-stealing markdowns of old goods, but by fresh new products which by now we all should recognize is the catalyst to increased revenue.

Secondly, we have resolved to sell said products more quickly—which translates into faster inventory turnover. Supporting this resolution is accurate open-to-buy by store and classification, properly timed deliveries, identification of hot-selling styles for timely re-orders when possible, and dealing with slow-selling inventory through stock balancing or in-season markdowns as soon as problems arise.

Added by-products to increased sales and faster turn are better margins, stronger cash flow, reduced operating expenses as a percentage of sales, and an elevated GMROI. Gross margin is enhanced for a simple reason: The newer the products, the greater likelihood of the product selling at full price. Every retailer should be cognizant of the fact that new goods, timed properly, have the best chance of selling quickly. Look at turnover in the simplest way possible: Several small invoices for deliveries on a consistent basis, versus a few large ones due all at once. If you can accomplish this, turnover cannot help but be improved (providing you are not a chronic over-buyer due to poor inventory planning, lack of discipline, or both). Operating expenses are expressed as a percentage of sales. When sales go up, operating expense percentage goes down, and net profit goes up. It's simple math. Gross margin return on investment (GMROI) increases due to additional gross margin dollars being generated through more profitable sales along with a lower average cost inventory. Again, simple arithmetic.

Just as the early Romans approached each new calendar cycle by looking both backwards and forwards, if we embrace the benefits gained through retrospect to help guide our future path, we will be better prepared to receive the challenges of the coming year.

Here's wishing you a happy, healthy and prosperous New Year!

_____

January/February 2012

The Importance of Proper Timing

---◆---

As the saying goes, "Timing Is Everything." This may be especially true for shoe retailers.

Although selecting the right vendors and styles at the right price points is very important, establishing ideal start ship and completion dates for the orders you write can be just as important.

Before buying for any new season, you need to know which vendors have been the most profitable, along with what styles and sizes sold best during the season. No doubt, you know which lines were *not* profitable and which items didn't sell. At first blush, the mistakes may seem apparent, but was the lackluster performance for these items really a result of the merchandise lacking appeal, or was it something else? In many cases there's a good chance that *"something else"* was the improper **timing of deliveries**.

Building orders and planning delivery dates based around peaks and valleys unique to each business is an essential component to a sound merchandise plan. Let's consider women's sandals as an example. A typical selling season is February through June. March, April and May represent the heart of the cycle with sales usually peaking in April depending on weather and location. February and June are referred to as "shoulder" months. In February, stores normally start building sandal inventory levels for the spring season. This year, due to an unseasonably mild winter, some stores have moved sandal deliveries up earlier to attract the fashion customer who buys early in the season when new offerings are first presented. Just because the calendar says it's January, doesn't mean people aren't thinking about spring. Fresh new merchandise that has recently arrived provides a welcome relief to the frequent shopper who has been inundated with aggressive promotional markdowns on last season's boots for the past several weeks. June is typically a clearance month for sandals even though "in-season" markdowns probably will be taken much earlier on poorly performing styles. Final markdowns are typically taken in late summer, although this past year several stores experienced good sandals sales much longer due to warm fall temperatures in a large part of the country.

Study the data

Start by running a vendor profitability report. You will want this report to rank the vendors in each classification according to sales volume, maintained margin, and turnover or sell through. If your POS system does not have a report similar to this, request it. It is perhaps **the** most important report you can run. This exercise will be very eye-opening and may provide the ammunition needed for future vendor negotiations. You should also be able to run a similar report for sizes, colors, and if you're up to it, price points. Divide your open-to-buy dollars by allocating them to the top vendors you think you will be using in each classification, being sure to leave uncommitted open-to-buy for reorders, fill-ins, new vendors, and promotional merchandise. Once this exercise is complete, you are ready to tackle the timing issue.

Next, consider some merchandising realities. Higher-priced merchandise normally sells earlier in the season, and lower-priced items generally sell later. Recognizing this fact in addition to understanding the selling cycle of the classification you are buying will help you determine how the inventory flow needs to be structured.

Remember that your customers like to see new merchandise just as much as your sales people enjoy selling it, which means you need a fresh flow of merchandise arriving throughout the season. Many retailers have a habit of front-loading, or landing most of the merchandise early in the season. The store may look great early on, but it can look equally as bad as the season matures with broken sizes on key styles dominating the assortment mix. Stores that front-load often commit so much of the OTB to early shipments that cash is not readily available for size fill-ins and off-price opportunities that may exist at season end. This practice slows inventory turnover, interrupts cash flow, and potentially restricts volume growth.

Many vendors offer price advantages or extra dating if you permit them to land merchandise early. This approach often backfires because the merchandise is picked over before the season begins. Moreover, the sales associates are tired of the merchandise before the season arrives. Another point to be made against getting the majority of the inventory at the beginning of the season is that if business does not pan out as planned, you already have an entire season's worth of stock. Had you written backup orders on key styles, you would have had much more flexibility in modifying or even canceling as a last resort.

Just as landing merchandise too early can be dangerous, so is landing it too late. Landing merchandise too late could be inviting markdowns because there is too little time remaining in the season to sell the goods at full price. This is the major reason why an in-store completion or cancellation date should be used on every order.

The final key to scheduling ideal delivery dates lives in the open-to-buy. Your open-to-buy should reflect planned receipts by month, over the course of the season. Once you receive your monthly open-to-buy, you can then create a percentage of planned receipts per month, instead of a lump sum amount. Your monthly open-to-buy will reflect current trends and consumer buying patterns as they unfold over the course of the season. An additional benefit is that your accounts payable will be easier to deal with, and your cash flow will better mirror your expenditures. Think in terms of several small invoices, as opposed to fewer large ones.

By following these simple steps, you will have a clear picture of how receipts should flow. The closer you adhere to planned delivery dates, the better your business will perform.

Remember: **Timing Is Everything!**

———————

March/April 2012

Heard This One Lately?
You'll Die Laughing—Not.

◆

I heard a joke the other day, it goes like this:

Do you know how to make a small fortune in the retail business? **Start with a large one!**

I know, it's a real knee-slapper, right? The only problem with this joke is that if it weren't so shockingly true in all too many cases, it just might be funny.

How many retailers do you know where this scenario applies? Perhaps you are even one of them. If so, ask yourself the following questions:

- How did you get into this position?

- Why are you content staying in the situation?

- What steps might you be able to take to change your situation?

I know of retailers who are in this difficult state and aren't even aware of it. They have become so comfortable with their complacency that they don't even realize there is a more prosperous way to live. How do you know true success if you have never experienced it—especially if you spend the majority of your day-to-day life dealing with negatives?

Reactive versus Proactive

I recently came across a situation where a retailer had gotten into a negative cash position. The majority of his time and energy was spent appeasing, coaxing, threatening, pleading and negotiating with vendors to take token payments on past due invoices. His hope was that his vendors might grant mercy in the form of some nominal credit extension that would allow him to land at least some new merchandise, the lifeblood of all retailers. This hand-to-mouth existence is no different than that of a drug addict who refuses treatment in favor of the next fix. It is clearly a short-term "solution" to a long-term problem.

To be fair, I am not suggesting for a moment that there aren't times for most retailers where cash flow is stronger than other times. Cash flow is a routine business concern. In the situation outlined above, any available cash reserves had been drained through a combination of poor merchandising decisions and even worse financial control. Generating cash needed to pay maxed-out credit cards and the line of credit that the bank wanted to reduce was being hindered by a costly store build-out, an unrealistic lease, and shrinking margins due to aggressive promoting. Declining sales, due to lack of fresh product, led to delayed deliveries caused by slow payments to vendors. The result was an inventory that was out of balance. The sales decrease forced the operating expense percentages to rise by default. Without intervention of some sort, this downward spiral will most likely continue until everything crashes. Ever seen it happen?

Many good retailers have seen it. The questions become: Who needs the stress? Is the business really worth all of this? You need someone to talk to, but whom? Look around at the possibilities. The vendors want you to pay what you already owe so they can ship you more, so they're out. Your accountant, bless his heart, is constantly reminding you of your dire position, but doesn't have the answers you need to solve the problem. Your spouse is weary of hearing about the store's problems and just wants you to do something, **anything**. You can't go to the employees with this, so you keep the happy face on, trying to seem positive. Hey, what about the banker? Forget it. He'll talk to you about money when you don't need it. And you certainly can't approach him with the current financials, because he might get freaked out and call your loan if you don't produce more collateral which you obviously don't have. You can't ask your family for more money—they are going to question your ability, perhaps even your sanity. You're putting in too many hours, not sleeping well, and becoming short with your friends and relatives.

There are solutions available.

One of the benefits of belonging to a trade association is that the Association has places and people to refer you to, should you find yourself dealing with "issues" from time to time. When seeking out a business consultant, mentor, or industry expert, do your homework. You will be spending some money to get the help you need, so make sure you are getting someone qualified to help. Look for an expert advisor who has industry experience, thoroughly understands your situation and can provide you with a concrete action plan that is realistic to you. Don't be afraid to ask for references, and follow through on contacting them.

I hear stories like the one I have discussed more often than I would like. Please forgive me if I fail to see the humor in the joke about making a small fortune by starting with a large fortune.

I have a better story:

Do you know how to make a large fortune in the retail business?

Start with a small one and don't be afraid to reach out for a second opinion if you think things could be better. There just might be a brighter future than you think.

May/June 2012

Which Definition Do You Use for "Expense"?

———————— ◆ ————————

ex.pense\ik-spen(t)s. a: something extended to secure a benefit or bring about a result b: financial burden or outlay.

Which definition properly describes an expense to you? Both definitions are correct, so how you answer the question is a matter of perception. This is one of those "Do you see the glass as half empty or half full?" questions. I encounter many retailers so overly concerned with part (b) that they never realize the possible benefits of (a). They just have a mental block relative to expenses, which unfortunately keeps them from progressing. These are the same folks that, time and time again, appear to step over dollars to pick up pennies.

Paying for Security

I can think of lots of things I pay a fee for that I would rather not. I bet you can, too. Tops on my list used to be insurance. Life, health, home, car, disability, umbrella, etc., all of the insurance options seem like they could go on forever. In fact, there are more than 150 different types of insurance policies that you can buy if you are so inclined. You can even insure your dog or cat if you want.

If we all had the ability to predict our futures, we could plan our lives accordingly and perhaps avoid insurance premiums altogether. Would that be nice? However, since most of us don't possess the ability to accurately predict life's day-to-day occurrences, we opt for the security of knowing that if life does present a problem, we can avoid a potentially hefty financial burden by being "covered" by insurance. Insurance is one of those things that most of us complain about paying for, until we actually need it—and then we are thankful we have it. In fact, if I didn't have to pay for home-owners insurance, I could have "saved" $1800 last year—but I also would have come out of pocket for $35,000 for a new roof that the insurance company covered due to hail damage. That one incident represented over nineteen years of premiums.

Do you really need a lease negotiator? Well, not if you own your building outright or perhaps have a background in commercial leasing. Anything short of that would make a lease negotiator a good idea and potentially save you thousands in the long run.

What Services Do You Need?

Do you really need an architect? How about a CPA? These services, among others, are integral pieces for the financial foundation of a retail operation. They all represent specific areas of expertise that save retailers money above and beyond the perceived *"expense."* Most prudent retailers wouldn't think of building a new store without the input of a qualified architect or store designer. Nor would they attempt to negotiate a lease on their own or navigate financial matters minus an accountant, or even open the doors without many types of insurance.

Another important part of any retailer's financial foundation is a sound inventory plan. Properly constructed, monitored and regularly updated, this tool is every bit as vital to the success of a retail operation as the other services mentioned. The merchandise plan provides the structure for all of the buying and selling. Since inventory is a retailer's largest asset, it stands to reason that time and resources should be allocated in this area. Most larger operations have a staff of planners who are responsible for developing, revising, and maintaining the merchandise plan. For many independent retailers, however, outsourcing the inventory forecasting function is a better business option which may make sense on several fronts.

Outsourcing Can Save Money

Outsourcing the planning function usually involves hiring a service bureau that specializes in this area. I am not referring to a POS company that happens to offer an OTB module almost as an afterthought, but rather a time-tested, results-oriented firm that delivers proven results. The cost of outsourcing pales in comparison to supporting an in-house planning department. First of all, with outsourcing there is no payroll expense, so therefore no added benefits expense. There is also no hidden agenda, as is often the case with intra-company planners. Service bureaus don't play politics, which means they therefore render the plan emotionally neutral with regard to company agendas. The consultant assigned to the account should be an independent, objective, third-party observer who brings an outside perspective void of emotion and family dynamics. He or she can draw from a wealth of experiences gained from other clients facing similar situations.

In addition to the cost savings and objective analysis, a good merchandise planning company should be able to quantify savings through improved inventory turnover, higher margins, stronger cash flow, better inventory balance and increased sales.

As a practical example, I personally have been working for nearly a year with a client that is enjoying a 13% sales increase and a 5% reduction in markdowns, and has trimmed the retail inventory by nearly $1,000,000. Suffice it to say, the "expense" of the outsourced merchandise planning function has paid for itself for the next several years, as well it should.

The next time you are presented with an expense, try reviewing it using the definition that includes part (a) as well as part (b). You just might find that those dollars you have been stepping over start going back into your checking account.

July/August 2012

A Winning Incentive Strategy For Sales Associates

---◆---

"Put that coffee down, coffee is for closers only!"
—ALEC BALDWIN IN "GLENGARRY GLEN ROSS"

One of my all-time favorite sales movies is the 1992 film "Glengarry Glen Ross." Anyone who is in or has been in a sales organization can perhaps relate to this film based on David Mamet's Pulitzer Prize-winning play. The film stars Al Pacino, Jack Lemmon, Alec Baldwin, Ed Harris, Alan Arkin, and Kevin Spacey. The star-studded cast alone is worth the Redbox rental fee. A word of caution is in order, however: The language is a bit rough and I wouldn't call this a "feel-good" movie. If you go forward, consider yourself warned. One of the most dramatic scenes is a new sales contest, where first prize is a new Cadillac Eldorado, second price is a set of steak knives, and third prize is "You're fired!" (Next line: "Have I got your attention now, I think I do?")

ABC: Always Be Closing

Since wage and salary expense makes up the second largest expense category for an independent shoe retailer, I thought it might be interesting to find out just exactly what retailers are doing to compensate and motivate sales associates. As part of my research, I took an informal poll of several retailers and discovered the following:

Hourly Rate: $8.00-$15.00

Discount: 30-50% on purchases, with some stores giving free shoes as often as "each season" to "annually."

Insurance: 50-90% paid by employer for health insurance for full-time employees in the stores that offer it.

Bonus: This area was so varied, it seems best to list a few examples.

- No goals, no bonuses.

- 1% commission paid if total store achieved a pre-set monthly sales goal.

- 6% bonus paid on the difference if last year's sales were exceeded by 20%.

- Various formulas involving multiple sales, average sale, number of items per ticket, foot scans, and additional sales of accessories including socks and insoles.

One retailer told me he paid $10 an hour vs. a 10% commission. He further explained, "If they are not making commission, they are not working here for long."

Jack Welch, the well-known former CEO of General Electric, was famous for terminating the bottom-producing 10% every year. Everyone knew the rules going in and it seemed to work for GE. I'm not suggesting that independent retailers adopt hard and fast rules that would result in head-rolling for 10% of the sales force, but with payroll costs running nearly 23%, the largest portion of which is selling costs, making up 10.6% (NSRA's *Business Performance Report 2011*), this is an area that needs monitoring.

Use the KISS Method

I believe in incentives. I believe that most people serving in a sales capacity are motivated by money. If they are not, they may still be good employees, but they are not serving in the right capacity. I believe in setting achievable goals that reward both the company and the employee. I believe compensation structures need to be as simple as possible, hence the KISS method, an acronym for "Keep It Simple, Stupid!" I believe in paying bonuses to sales associates for contributions above and beyond the minimum expectations, not for showing up and "punching the clock." I believe that people have different skill sets, personalities, and motivation that might affect how much they make. I subscribe to what I might best describe as a Darwinist approach, in that I believe the more you sell, the more value you add to the organization and the more you should make. It's simple and it's fair.

"A man only hits what he aims for.", reads a sign on the wall of Premiere Properties in the movie "Glengarry Glen Ross."

I would like to offer an approach that not only provides incentive to sales people, but is also designed to reduce selling costs at the same time, resulting in a win-win formula. Assume the following:

Hours/Week	15.0
Base Hourly Wage	$10.00
Monthly Sales	$10,500.00
Weeks/Month	4.0
Base Selling Cost	10%
Commission Rate (for Sales Over Base)	5%

Now do the math:

15.0 Hours Worked/Week x 4.0 Weeks/Month = 60.0 Hours Worked/Month

$10.00 Base Hourly Wage x 60.0 Hours Worked/Month = $600.00

Base Salary of $600 ÷ Selling Cost of 10% = $6,000 (Base)

$10,500.00 Actual Sales/Month – $6,000 the Base = Sales Over Base of $4,500

In this example, a selling cost of 10% is used to determine a base; in this case, it is $6000. No commission is paid until the base is reached. Once achieved, a 5% commission is paid on all sales volume over base. The sales associate earns more based on what he or

Commission Rate for Sales Over Base 5%
Commission on Sales Over Base = $225.00

Total Monthly Wages	$825.00
Actual Sales/Month	$10,500.00
Actual Selling Cost = 7.86%	

Total Monthly Wages	$825.00
Hours Worked/Month	60
Total Hourly Wages = $13.75	

120

she sells and the selling costs go down accordingly.

So go ahead, have that coffee now because everybody is a winner with this strategy!

———————————

September/October 2012

You Can Only Fire Me Once!

— ◆ —

A large volume store recently came to us with an interesting dilemma. The store had a good gross margin and a fabulous inventory turnover, yet was not making any money.

The merchant had a gross margin of 48% and operating expenses of the same. Not surprisingly, the store accountant's initial reaction was to mandate that $1,000,000 be cut from operating expenses immediately. So the accounting minions went to work examining every line item on the expense budget to see where cuts could in fact be made. Rents were examined and renegotiated where possible, selling expenses were more ardently monitored, and the scalpel was taken to the advertising and promotion budget as well. Travel, freight, insurance, outside services, you name it, were scrutinized.

Careful review and control of operating expenses is prudent for every retailer. The exercise however, is a one-trick pony. You can only fire someone once! In other words, once an expense is cut, it's cut. No retailer can continue to back into a strong profit and loss statement by continually chopping expenses. A retailer typically gets one pass at this strategy, after which merchandising performance must improve in order to grow.

If you take the engine out of a car, it will make the car lighter. That is true, the car will have less weight, but won't be able to move. So the objective of reducing the car's weight is achieved, but in doing so the car is not able to function as designed. The same concept is true when reducing operating expenses. Selling costs that are too aggressively cut will end up costing the company sales. Trimming the ad budget by too much can lead to lack of visibility in the marketplace. Cut out travel and pretty soon, the store risks not showing the newest products available. The examples are endless. You can trim the fat only so far before cutting into muscle. You will need to find another way to increase profitability. Reductions in operating expenses may serve to accomplish a short-term profit goal, but the strategy is not sustainable in the long run. You ultimately will need to increase sales volume.

Back to our example: The assumptions we made were that the majority of the major expenses, once trimmed, were for all practical purposes "fixed" expenses as opposed to "variable" expenses which adjust according to sales. We also were convinced that the store was able to maintain the same margin on any planned sales increase.

We knew the margins were reasonable and the forty million dollar sales volume was no small piece of change. So where was the problem? A peak "under the hood" at the merchandising data showed that the store was turning its inventory way too quickly and losing thousands of dollars in sales in some classifications.

Turn Fast—or Too Fast?

Any regular reader of this column knows that I extol the virtues of faster turns at every opportunity. The benefits of faster turns have been discussed on many previous occasions. There is, however, a balance that must be struck between turning too quickly and missing business, and not turning fast enough and having cash flow and markdown issues. This optimum balance can only be achieved if you regularly monitor the sales and inventory plan at the store and classification level.

In this case, a 5% sales increase, deemed easily attainable by slowing the turn in areas where business was being missed, proved to be a viable solution. By reviewing the sales and inventory forecast monthly with this retailer, we were able to show him how his inventory dollars could best be allocated to achieve the volume increase he needed. By adding inventory in the right classifications at the right time we *purposely* slowed the turnover in order to maximize sales. Margins and operating expense *dollars* remained constant, the increase in volume yielding a 2.4% improvement in net profit. Any expense reduction possible only makes the end result that much better.

Get a Check-Up

Every retailer should periodically have a "check-up." Much can be learned by allowing an independent third party to objectively review the merchandising data, as well as the financials. This simple process generally involves emailing sales, inventory and profit and loss information. Generally, all that is needed is a couple of screen shots from most POS systems. When I do an analysis, I try to get information at the class level if possible. The most rewarding part of the process is when I am able to discover areas of upside potential buried deep within a retailer's data. To me, this is like a big treasure hunt. Once the opportunities are discovered, a plan of action is agreed upon and set into motion. The puzzle is solved.

_____

November/December 2012

The Great Debate: Markdown or Carryover?

———————————— ◆ ————————————

No single question has been posed to me more often. Retailers of all types always seem to question whether they would be financially better off to mark down and clear out remaining past season inventory, or to carry it over for the same season next year. In the shoe industry, this topic arises twice a year, in late summer at the end of sandal season and in late winter/early spring when boot sales are winding down.

Outlining the Argument

The argument for carryover generally involves a merchant not wanting to heavily discount products that he or she feels will have to be repurchased next year. These products will be, in most cases, the same styles and colors as the previous year. Prices may be higher, which provides the retailer a chance to even mark **up** the existing stock to reflect current retail prices, therefore generating perhaps even more gross margin dollars than the previous year.

The case for clearing out seasonal merchandise is structured around generating cash flow from goods that did not sell during the period for which they were intended. Open-to-buy for the category is not compromised by trying to "buy around" past season's carryover. Colors sometimes *do* change, styles often *are* updated, boxes *do* get worn, merchandise tags *can* become frayed and discolored, not to mention ancillary expenses such as taxes and insurance that will be incurred on old inventory.

Considerations

Perhaps the first question you must ask yourself is, "Why is there extra inventory in the first place?" In the case of the winter of 2011-12, warm weather precluded several retailers from selling as many boots, gloves, hats, and other cold-weather items as they may have sold during a "normal" winter. Was this the entire story or a symptom of a bigger problem such as a poorly designed merchandise plan (or, worse yet, no plan)? Another consideration would be to evaluate your current cash needs. Ask yourself, "Do I want the cash from this inventory now, or can I afford to sit on it in my backroom for six months and hope I sell it the next season?" A good follow up question at this point might be, if you didn't sell the particular item last season, why do you think demand will be any stronger next year? Will your customers notice or care that you are dragging out last year's merchandise?

Look at the Numbers

Example A: Sales of winter boots for the year are $100,000 with a gross margin of 48% or $48,000. The boot classification turns 2.5 times.

$100,000/2.5 turns = $40,000 average inventory @ retail.

$40,000 x 52% (cost compliment of the GM) = $20,800 average inventory @ cost.

GMROI = $48,000/$20,800=$2.3 GMROI

Example B: Sales of winter boots for the year are $100,000. Gross margin= 42% or $42,000. Turns are 4.

$100,000/4 turns = $25,000 average inventory @ retail.

$25,000 x 58% = $14,500 average inventory @ cost.

GMROI = $42,000/$14,500 = $2.9 GMROI

(NOTE: GMROI is gross margin return on investment. In calculating GMROI, gross margin dollars are divided by average inventory at cost.)

In the illustration above, sales are the same for both examples. In Example A, markdowns are nominal and inventory turnover for a seasonal class is slow. Space doesn't allow for a 12-month merchandise plan of this class to be viewed or you would see that more merchandise was carried over in the off months than would be optimal. Inventory actually sat on the shelves for nearly five months with no sales activity. In Example B, markdowns were taken throughout the season on slow-moving styles and end of season markdowns were more significant. The result was $6,000 less in gross margin dollars. The faster turn came from the fact that inventory levels started building in August, peaked in October, and stock was virtually gone by March. The end result is an increase in GMROI of 26%.

As a general rule, it makes more sense to clean up seasonal offerings and buy fresh the next year. That said, your world won't come crashing down and you won't be viewed by your peers as a terrible retailer if you decide there are a few styles hither and yon that, for whatever reason, you feel you can't part with. What must be avoided at all costs are backrooms crammed with seasonal carryover year after year, tying up needed cash, and choking off the ability to land fresh new products—which we all know is the driving force behind increased sales.

_____

January/February 2013

Pareto's Principle: The 80/20 Rule

◆

In 1906, an Italian economist by the name of Vilfredo Pareto created a mathematical formula describing the unequal distribution of wealth in his country. He observed that 80% of the wealth, which was mostly land at that time, was owned by 20% of the people. In the 1930s and '40s, quality manager pioneer Dr. Joseph Juran recognized the universal applications that the "law of the vital few" had and applied it to business. Thus Pareto's Principle—or the 80/20 rule, as it would be known—was born.

Examples of the 80/20 rule in the retail world are numerous:

- 20% of the vendors you carry supply 80% of the inventory you have.

- 80% of your sales come from 20% of your stock.

- 80% of the sales are produced by 20% of the sales associates.

- 20% of the staff causes 80% of the problems.

- 80% of your time is spent dealing with the 20%.

Though the 80/20 examples above may perhaps not be absolute for your company, the idea is to understand that the principle exists and it can be used to manage more effectively.

Some popular management theories suggest that the most effective use of time, talent, and resources is to focus almost entirely on further development of the 20% that is already performing and leave the remaining

80% status quo. With regard to inventory management, I would offer that efforts to improve the 80% would prove more beneficial.

Overstocked While Understocked

Let's assume that we have a classification where 80% of the sales are coming from 20% of the inventory, a very common scenario. Most often, I see this in a class that is overstocked and under stocked at the same time. Usually contributing to the overstock situation is old, dated inventory consisting of broken sizes, discontinued styles, poor color choices and even vendors that are no longer part of the merchandise assortment. In other words, the class consists of **a whole lot of nothing**. Typically, the same class will be understocked on items that are selling well and should be filled in, but are not because "on paper" the class is overbought. This class will never reach full potential until this problem is diagnosed and remedied. Typical merchandising benchmarks of turn, margin, GMROI, can oftentimes be misleading if not thoroughly reviewed. In my opinion, this is the very reason that shoe stores as a group have historically never experienced turns faster than 2-2.2 times.

Take a hypothetical classification with ten styles. Let's assume that two of the styles have just been received and are blowing off the shelves. Let's further assume that five styles are just OK and that three styles are real dogs. In fact, they are so bad that you had to check the purchase order to see if you *really* bought them in the first place. If the store is functioning efficiently, the fast-selling styles get reordered immediately, the "dogs" get returned or marked down just as quickly, and the so-so styles are scrutinized closely throughout the selling season. If you are reviewing at the class level only, and not drilling down to the SKU level in your POS system, you may miss the hot sellers and the "dogs." This is the very reason that good POS systems allow you to create fast and slow seller reports.

If the reorders get missed, sales begin to suffer because sizes become depleted and remaining styles are not as desirable. If the "dog" styles are not dealt with immediately by way of a vendor return or early in-season markdowns, inventory levels become bloated, slowing turnover and choking off open-to-buy.

Narrow and Deep

In theory, the cash generated from marking down the slow-selling styles pays for the reorders of the faster-selling ones. As the store approaches the peak of the selling season, the assortment of styles offered at the beginning of the season would have narrowed, while the styles in demand would be readily available in needed sizes and colors. If the store has effectively managed its open-to-buy plan, it should now be in a position to land promotional merchandise to blend into the assortment at season end. If you are lucky or if you have negotiated well with the vendor upfront, you might be able to buy the same styles that performed well during the season at a promotional price. This merchandise will serve to boost both sales and margins for the category.

Managing the 80/20 rule is a continual process. The value of the Pareto Principle is that it continually reminds us to focus not only on the 20% that is the driving force behind the sales, but also to manage the remaining 80% more efficiently.

If you accept the premise behind the 80/20 rule, then 20% of the people receiving this magazine will end up reading this article. If you have gotten this far, you are part of the 20%. Out of this group, 20% will actually **do** something proactive relative to this concept while 80% will not. And so it goes.

If you are among the select 20%, congratulations! Try shifting some of your focus to the 80% not working for you and see how quickly things improve.

March/April 2013

A 12-Step Program
for Overbuying

———————————— ◆ ————————————

Are you a chronic overbuyer? Over the past thirty plus years of working with independent retailers, I have become convinced that the continual practice of buying more than one can profitably sell is an addiction.

If you engage in financially destructive merchandising behavior season after season, year after year, with the best of intentions, only to end up enduring the same disappointing results, this article may be a lifesaver. If this scenario applies to you, be aware that you are not alone. Misery loves company and you certainly have lots of it. The good news is that, with a little help, the success rate of recovery is quite good.

I have developed a recovery program for retailers who find themselves members of this group from time to time. The test below identifies some of the warning signs of chronic overbuying. See how you score by grabbing a sheet of paper and jotting down your "yes" or "no" to each question:

- Do you often feel forced to markdown merchandise to generate cash to pay invoices?

- Do you struggle with cash flow issues regularly?

- Do you experience slow shipments because you owe vendors money?

- Do your customers "wait you out" because they know your store has huge sales?

- Have you ever heard customers say that your store always has "the best sales?"

The 12-Step Overbuying Recovery Program:

Step 1: Admit you have a buying problem and that it has become unmanageable.

Step 2: Accept that there is an answer outside of your store that can guide you in the right direction.

Step 3: Once you have found what you believe is the guidance your operation needs, make a decision and move forward.

Step 4: Implement a sales and inventory plan by store and classification—and stick to it.

Step 5: Learn to say "NO!" if the line doesn't appeal to you. Remember, it's your money.

Step 6: Review your merchandise-on-order report monthly at the very least.

Step 7: Don't allow substitutions without your prior approval, and don't accept goods past completion date without a discount.

Step 8: Change the misguided belief that in all cases you need more to sell more.

Step 9: Re-trend your sales forecast regularly. Look for breakout classifications as well as areas beginning to slow.

Step 10: Avoid the naysayers. These are the people that want to keep you locked in the old behavior.

Step 11: Reduce the amount of preseason orders. This is where the problems start. You know you are going to need money to fill in hot sellers as well as some promotional buys.

Step 12: Don't be too hard on yourself. Relapses can happen and you are likely to fall off the wagon more than once. Stay the course. This is a career-long solution.

- Is it important to you that your reps like you no matter what?

- Does your floor or backroom ever feel over-crowded with merchandise?

- Do you ever run out of places to display merchandise?

- Do you find yourself canceling orders every season?

- Do you ever buy close-outs because you can't pass up a "good deal" even though you already have too much inventory?

- Do you ever feel pressure to buy because a rep has taken the time to show you a line?

- Do you buy what you like and hope it is the right amount?

Now, total your "yes" and "no" answers. An occasional "yes" answer to the questions above is probably no cause for concern. However, if you answered in the affirmative to six or more, this could be a sign of trouble.

Continued overbuying can be a destructive behavior. I have seen it harm relationships, reduce credit ratings, and destroy businesses. Like most addictions, overbuying is treatable. The key point is that you get help. Not unlike other recovery programs, **you** must take the first step. The 12-step program outlined at right is adapted from other highly recognizable and successful programs. I have modified it to be applicable to the retail industry.

Of all the steps outlined at left, step 10 might just be the most challenging. If you are the company president or owner, you are constantly surrounded by enablers. These are the people that like you the way you were *before*. In many cases (not all obviously, but several), vendor reps are the biggest enablers. They don't want you to change. The more you overbuy, the more money they make. This is a great example of codependent behavior. Your own customers can be enablers. You will hear it in their comments, including "We used to just love your sales," or my favorite, "Are you going out of business? You don't have as much merchandise as you did before." This comment can be frightening for some retailers until they get comfortable with the process. The store's buyers can be enablers. Buying by classification takes getting used to. It's a new skill and buyers are creatures of habit. They are not fond of change. They will tell you they like things better "the old way," which was when buyers had free rein and could buy what they wanted, when they wanted, without accountability. Make no mistake: This 12-step program is all about accountability.

May/June 2013

Cash Flow:
The New Financial Reality

◆

As a retailer, what is more important to you, profits or cash flow? The initial response from most merchants posed that question is: "Profits, of course!"

On the surface, that answer makes sense; who wouldn't want more profits? The mere word "profitable" itself evokes a sense of financial well-being. In today's retail environment, though, profits alone are not enough; **cash flow** is the new financial reality.

I have reviewed countless profit and loss statements that showed extremely strong gross margin figures, only to find out that the store had no cash. Since accounting does not factor in the element of time, turnover does not appear on a profit and loss statement. Therefore, the financial picture created by a "profitable" business with poor cash flow can be a false reality.

Recently, a client came to us for a strategy to deal with a bank request. The bank wanted the retailer to produce an additional $200,000 in cash, not profits—cash. If you were given a similar mandate, what would you do? Well, hope is not a strategy and crying is not an option. To paraphrase Tom Hanks' famous line about baseball from the film, "A League of Their Own," **There is no crying in retail.** Three more practical solutions quickly come to mind: Cut expenses, increase sales or cut inventory. Let's examine all three.

Option: Cutting Expenses

Putting excess expenses on the chopping block is an obvious first step to save some cash. The problem here is that most retailers feel they have already trimmed expenses to the bone. If you have recently renegotiated your leases, reviewed payroll costs, and scrutinized the remaining administrative costs, there may not be much left to cut.

Slashing costs too deeply can actually have a negative effect on business. Several "big box" retailers have experienced this recently as sales have been undermined by deep cuts in staffing and training. Prudence and caution are priorities when examining expenses.

Option: Increase Sales

Increasing sales sounds like a viable option, but how? You can promote more, but you might experience a margin hit which will most certainly raise a banker's eyebrows. You could buy more inventory, which *might* drive volume, but the risk is that the cash problem could worsen if the additional stock does not perform as it should. You could advertise more, but that would only increase expenses if the ad campaign didn't pull enough customers in.

Option: Cut Inventory

The third option is to cut inventory. Cleaning out excess stock will generate more cash in the short term. The dilemma, however, is how to consistently build cash over the long term. I prefer the scalpel approach as opposed to the meat cleaver method. Anybody can slash and burn inventory and generate quick cash, but the aftermath of kneejerk business decisions can haunt you for months to come. This is the very reason that I object so strongly to the marketing strategy of 20% off everything in the store, or what is often referred to as "the lazy man's markdown."

This promotional approach does little to solve merchandising problems, since the desirable items that *could* have sold at full price are the first to sell at discounted prices. Aside from a momentary bump in cash, the downside is reduced margins and broken size runs. Worst of all, the problem inventory is still a problem.

A Better Answer

Strategic planning is the answer. This means bottom up dollar merchandise planning at the store and class level. Most often a retailer's line of credit (LoC) is tied to inventory. A banker's valuation of inventory is what he thinks he can liquidate it for given the outside chance that the bank ends up with the keys to the store.

Because of the way bankers perceive the value of inventory, they get nervous whenever the word "cutting" is mentioned. Understand that to a banker, goods that are a year or two old have the same value as merchandise that was received yesterday. In most cases (although not all), what the banker sees with regard to your inventory is *only* numbers on a financial statement. Given their reference point, it is understandable, though not always justifiable, why a lending institution might require more collateral when stock levels are reduced. For that reason, it is paramount that you keep the communication channels wide open with the bank if you depend on them for your LoC. Demonstrate to bankers, using sales and inventory reports, that fresh, "balanced" inventory has a better chance of increasing sales than simply having more inventory. It is also a good idea to have your banker visit your store and even attend a management or buying meeting. Treat the banker as part of your management team.

Anyone working in the retail business longer than a week knows the positive effect that new products can have on sales when received at the proper time. Customers don't visit your store to see what came in last year. It is the constant flow of fresh inventory that drives profitable sales. A strategic merchandise plan that blends inventory balance with properly scheduled deliveries, and timely markdowns, is the pathway to faster turnover, which drives sales volume.

There are few problems in retail that can't be remedied by increasing sales and cash flow. Hence, my new retail math formula: **Cash Flow + Sales Increases = No Problems!**

_____

July/August 2013

Do You Suffer From
Analysis Paralysis?

◆

Today's information technology is so comprehensive that some retailers are not taking full advantage of the knowledge available to them. Too often I see retailers make big investments on elaborate systems that end up being used for little more than expensive ticket printing machines with cash drawers or printing presses for volumes of reports that are seldom used.

Take the case of a large Latin American multi-store shoe retailer we know. They knew they had an inventory problem and needed to reduce stock levels by 20%. Since all of the corporate planning was being done top down, 20% cuts were mandated across the board. The immediate results were disastrous and here's why. The only data piece visible to management was a top down view of sales at the class level across all stores. A total company view, if you will. I would equate this to solving a ground floor problem from 5,000 feet up. In actuality, the merchant did have availability to the proper tools, but didn't know how to accurately interpret the information or how to implement a successful strategy.

The end result was that good-performing stores in the chain that desperately needed product, endured inventory reductions of 20%, which immediately stopped sales growth. Poor performers also received stock reductions, but not always in the right areas, leading to even weaker performance.

Once our team was able to gain visibility at the classification level by store, we quantified to management exactly how much business was being lost in all of the stores by using the current inventory reduction strategy.

The good news is that given an accurate merchandise plan and proper guidance, this retailer was able to re-balance inventory, supplying fresh new merchandise to the stores needing it. Older styles, sizes and colors that had been one of the major causes of the inventory problem initially were identified and marked for immediate clearance. This new strategy accomplished many positives. First, slow sellers were dealt with aggressively, releasing much-needed cash into the organization. Secondly, the new cash was used to chase hot-selling styles, which raised sales. Thirdly, margins increased because the merchant now had visibility at the store and class level to what was and was not working. Class level information coupled with vendor performance and style selling reports helped them target trouble spots without taking blanket markdowns on an entire class of merchandise, or for that matter the entire store. This is what I have termed "The Lazy Markdown."

The Lazy Markdown

This is a markdown strategy used by some retailers in an attempt to generate increased traffic and quick cash, both of which are in most cases short-term solutions to longer-term merchandising issues. You can see examples of the Lazy Markdown by opening your local paper or simply walking down Main Street. The ad or sign in the window will read something like this: "20% Off Everything in the Store!"

This is, in most cases, a knee-jerk act of desperation. The sign might as well read, "Help! I need cash fast!"

The usual results are that the prime inventory is "creamed," with the best styles, sizes and colors being quickly snatched up. What is left is broken size runs of good sellers and complete size runs of styles that the retailer was hoping to move in the first place. Aside from perhaps seasonal clearance times, there is one time this type of sale should be used: when you are starting your "Going Out of Business Sale!" A more effective strategy would be to target the trouble spots and be more aggressive with the discount. Remember the old adage, "The first markdown is the cheapest,"? That's true—as long as it works.

Drinking Out of a Fire Hose

Today, even smaller and less sophisticated POS systems can provide retailers a level of detailed information that in previous generations one could only imagine. Unless you know what you are looking for, where to find the information, how to interpret the data, and how to set up an action plan, the flow of information can quickly become akin to trying to drink out of a fire hose.

Superfluous reports generated simply because you have access to data which doesn't have a positive impact on your business are meaningless. Employ the KISS method (Keep It Simple, Stupid) whenever possible; the simpler, the better. Separate the **need to know** from the **nice to know** and you will be able to make better use of your system. Some of the best merchants I know use only a fraction of the data that their systems are capable of generating.

Get Training

Most likely you have invested a great deal of money, time and manpower in your current system. Sometimes you have had to do this more than once before getting it right. For heaven's sake, make certain that you understand the functionality of the system. I hear too many retailers complaining about their POS systems when they haven't fully taken the time to learn all of the capabilities. True, some systems are better than others and all systems have strengths and weaknesses. By this point, your investment in the POS system is a "sunk cost" so make the most of it.

Analysis Paralysis

With the amount of data available from today's systems, it is easy for some merchants to fall victim to a syndrome I call "analysis paralysis." This is recognizable by the merchant who analyzes data six ways from Tuesday yet still makes poor buying decisions. Worse yet is the person who can't or won't make a decision until they "run more reports." This reminds me of the golfer who shows up on the first tee with the best equipment and the most fashionable outfit, takes ten practice swings before every shot, yet can't hit the ball. Focus on the areas that will give you the greatest return. Do reasonable quantitative research and take action. It *ain't* rocket science, so don't make it that. Buy the best, and pass the rest.

September/October 2013

"Everyone Has a Plan until They Get Punched in the Mouth."

———————— ◆ ————————

I am guessing that heavyweight boxer Mike Tyson never saw himself as a business philosopher, but he certainly didn't pull any punches with this quote. The analogy between his quote and the trials and tribulations of the retail business is about as good as it gets.

Most retailers approach planning for the upcoming year by reviewing what happened the previous year, good or bad. Modifications are made, taking into account the weather, the economy, the political landscape, merchandise trends, and current vendor relationships, among other factors. Depending on the size and sophistication of the operation, the planning process can be as basic as an owner preparing a plan by himself, or as complex as soliciting input from a variety of sources including buyers, financial control folks, merchandise managers and even store operations staff.

Planning is most often done in the privacy of an office, surrounded by supporting spreadsheets and reports intended to back up or reinforce the outcome. It's well and good to this point. Assuming the plan is constructed accurately, taking into account trends in classification sales, margins, turnover rates, proper timing of deliveries, and so on, reasonable results could be expected. However, much like a boxing match, the retail environment stands ready to deliver "punches to the mouth" sufficient enough to knock even the strongest of merchants down for the count if they have not prepared to go the distance.

Unanticipated—and Dramatic

Getting punched in the mouth is analogous to the unanticipated events that can have dramatic effects on a business plan. Weather, like a boxing opponent, is unpredictable and capable of delivering a sucker punch to the best of plans. Warm, dry winters can bruise a boot season just like cold, wet springs hurt sandal sales. If these two seasons occur back to back, it's a right, left combination that can land a retailer on the ropes.

Other "punches" retailers endure might include late shipments (for any variety of reasons), road construction in front of the store, the best salesperson leaving, the landlord raising the rent, the air conditioning going out on the first hot day, fit issues, shoplifting, the POS system becoming obsolete, and on and on. Any of many situations can be a huge body blow to the business.

How you recover from the many varied body blows you are bound to receive during the course of a year speaks volumes to how well you have planned. If the sales forecast is not trended properly, you run the risk of having either too much or too little inventory, the crucial starting point for any merchandise plan. If the turnover rate for the particular classification being planned is incorrect, the result could be missed sales opportunities or too much stock. Seasonal adjustments must be made to the planned inventory levels so as to have enough to meet customer demand, but not so much as to create a markdown problem. Exit strategies must be planned for clearance of seasonal products to avoid excessive carryover. Not having such a strategy can result in a blow below the belt, causing cash flow to be tight and, in severe cases, credit issues with vendors. Tight cash flow, in turn, can force a retailer to resort to alternative funding sources such as credit cards or tapping bank credit lines.

Build It into the Plan

Since markdowns affect sales as well as ending inventory levels, they should be built into the plan profitably at this time. Planned markdowns add to needed inventory. If sales and inventory projections are not met or were planned incorrectly, the business will experience yet another jab. Next is to plan the receiving flow at cost and retail. For this to be accurate, you will need to know the initial mark-up for each class. Finally, the merchandise-on-order expected is added for each store and class and you have your merchandise plan. One last kidney punch is possible, however. If all of the orders are not entered into the POS system, the open-to-buy will be wrong and you could end up buying too much.

Successful planning on both the merchandise side as well as the expense side is vital to any retail operation. Without a solid plan in place, the chances of success are greatly diminished. Creating a plan that relies on optimal business conditions or best-case scenarios is risky at best—and potentially disastrous at worst. Remember, it's not **if** you are going to get punched in the mouth this year; it's **when, how many times,** and **how hard**. With a solid plan, your business will be better prepared to go the distance. Those that chose not to plan might just be the ones that end up throwing in the towel.

_____

November/December 2013

Buy the Best, Pass the Rest

♦

Have you ever been in a situation where you pulled up to a stop light to discover that you will be spending the next two minutes of your life emotionally involved with an individual holding a sign that depicts the life challenges he or she is struggling with? The signs typically read something like, "homeless, please help," or "hungry and out of work" or anything designed to get you to roll down the window and part with some of your hard earned cash.

Consider the Options

You have options to consider during these very lengthy seconds. One is, you can do your best to avoid eye contact altogether. This is nearly impossible when the poor soul is standing a mere three feet from your driver's side door. You can stare back in defiance, wishing meanwhile that this societal blight wasn't tolerated in your city. After all, you work hard for your money, you know there are jobs available, and this guy is just looking for a handout. The most popular option, however, is to succumb to whatever guilt you are feeling, roll down the window and hand over the spare change or couple of bucks you can quickly grab from your wallet. You may say, "There you go." You may think this small problem goes away (for now). You have a temporary reprieve from guilt and you have "helped" someone less fortunate. But you really haven't helped anyone, have you? You did this for yourself so you would no longer feel uncomfortable.

"Solution" to a Struggle?

When I visit stores that are over-assorted and overstocked, I know the store's buyer(s) struggled with the same feelings as the person at the stop light. The buyers either can't follow their merchandise plan or don't have a solid plan to begin with. What generally ends up happening is, they roll down the window (figuratively) and throw little token orders to lots of vendors. They assume this will make all the reps like them and everybody will be happy.

Buying a little from everybody simply because someone has taken the time to show you a line or come into your store is really like rolling down the car window and handing the guy on the curb a few dollars. **It does nothing to help either party.** The vendors are the ones holding the signs that say "Please buy my line." You give them an order not because you really want that merchandise—you do it because you don't want to feel bad about turning someone down.

The ramifications of this practice are costly to your store and to the vendor. With a token order, you mean nothing to the resource and the resource means nothing to you. From the vendor's point of view, a line can't be properly represented and developed in this fashion. On the retailer's side, the merchandise that you really wouldn't have purchased in the first place probably doesn't fit into your assortment plan—and most likely is a duplication of something already carried. The merchandise becomes "lost in the sauce," ties up floor space and cash, slows your turnover and eventually reduces your margin when you wake up and mark it down. You are way better off to skip the line altogether than to write token orders for the wrong reasons.

Create a Resource Matrix

A seasoned merchant will avoid this situation by having a solid dollar control plan and a resource matrix that is consistent with the store's image. This is not to say that new lines shouldn't be continually tested. To the contrary, testing a concept, a new vendor, or a different price point is something that may develop into a viable business opportunity. We always want to reserve open-to-buy dollars available for these occasions.

Remember, it is more prudent to say "No" sometimes than it is to say "Yes" every time. Your job as a buyer is to select the merchandise that best represents what your customers are most likely to be willing to purchase and that stays in line with the image of your store. You will sell more with a focused presentation—and avoid assortment creep—if you "**Buy the Best and Pass the Rest!**"

July/August 2014

Be Honest with Yourself:
Are You a "Low Performer"?

◆

I think everybody, if truly honest, would like to think of themselves as something more than just "average." "Average," after all, is considered mediocre, middle-of-the-road, and often nondescript. Clearly, however, in NSRA's *Business Performance Report (BPR)* terms, not every store—or every employee—will be classified as a "high performer."

The most recent *BPR* sets forth retail metrics which it breaks down into categories of "high performers" and "low performers." I personally know many of NSRA's "high performers" and am proud of the fact that several of them are RMSA clients. To them I say, "Congratulations; keep raising the bar, moving the needle, and pushing the envelope. You are excused from reading the rest of this article."

I want to speak directly to those stores that might fall into the average or low performer category. Few people know the stores that live in this group. These aren't the folks that you meet at a trade show or an NSRA event; people at those events do not readily admit to performing on the sub-par side of industry norms.

The Ultimate Goal

Nobody goes into the shoe business—or any other kind of business—with the ultimate goal of being a low performer (LP). I think they end up being an LP for a variety of circumstances, some of which are outside of their control and some not. I believe they don't want to see themselves as "average." In fact, I doubt that most "low" performers are lazy, unmotivated, or untalented.

However, I **do** believe that mediocrity can become an acceptable norm if left unchallenged season after season, year after year. This, in my opinion, is a major difference between high performers and low performers.

I contend that there are reasons that some stores purposefully accept their low performer status. Those reasons include fear, reluctance to change, ego, control, lack of knowing what resources are available, and not wanting anyone else to know their business (usually because it's bad).

Fear of Change

When a retailer is held back by fear of change, many times the retailer is in a family business. You often hear the reasoning, "We've always done it this way," without hearing a convincing argument as to why the particular behavior is allowed to continue. To some folks, change can be frightening. In some cases, people are reluctant to "look under the hood" because they are afraid of what they might find and what course of action they might have to undertake to make things better.

I knew of a young man who put off seeing a doctor for over a year even though he had the classic symptoms of colon cancer. He rationalized his decision through a daily regimen of exercise designed to convince himself that he was "OK." Besides, he told himself, he was way too young and "healthy" for cancer. To make a long story short, he had a portion of his colon removed and endured a year's worth of chemotherapy, all of which involved considerable discomfort and may have been avoided if warning signs had been heeded and help sought earlier. Why didn't he seek help sooner? He later admitted that he didn't want to hear that something might be wrong with him. Had he waited much longer, he could have ended up as a "Permanent *Markdown!*" I know: Crazy, right? I say that lightly, not because anyone should take cancer lightly, but because sometimes a little lightness is a better way to make a memorable and important point.

The Verbal Excuses

Ego, arrogance and control are paranoia traits usually rooted in embarrassment or shame. We've all heard people say one or more of the following things:

- "I don't need outside help."

- "Nobody knows my business better than me."

- "We're different."

- "I don't want anybody to know my business."

- "Our store is unique."

Pardon my skepticism, but, "Yeah, right!" I can't tell you how many stores I have seen that have failed to maximize their upside potential—or, worse, go out of business because they were too stubborn, arrogant, or insecure to ask for help.

Taking no action is a cognitive business decision. All too often, refusing to act leads to a long list of economic calamities including lost jobs, abandoned lease obligations, unresolved vendor debt, and personal financial upheaval. Becoming a "high performer" starts with a state of mind and a personal commitment to become one.

Getting to a Higher Level

If you can honestly say that you want to get to a higher performance level, there are several steps you can—and should—take. Among them:

- Find advisors you can speak with honestly—whether they are bankers, accountants, fellow business owners, retired business owners, attorneys, former classmates or others. They have experience you can tap, in confidence.

- Read business books and magazines, and sit in on business discussions and presentations.

- Attend conferences and **listen**. You may not agree with other people's suggestions, but hearing what they think may spark you to think in a new direction.

- Go to trade shows and **watch**. See what excites other people, and try to figure out why.

- Hire outside help to take a realistic look at your business model and numbers. Somewhere in your network, there is an outside resource. You may find that resource through your Chamber of Commerce, another local business association, or a colleague.

As a business person myself, I would be remiss if I didn't remind you that RMSA, as an educational partner of NSRA, is here to help. However, there is one big problem: We don't know who you are. If you are feeling stuck, or consider yourself "average" but want to step up and become a "high performer," or fear you are falling short of industry benchmarks, I encourage you to reach out. With RMSA, all correspondence is confidential and there is no cost or obligation to discuss your particular situation and possible courses of action. If RMSA is not the ideal choice for you, we don't take it personally. We simply urge you to be the best owner you are capable of becoming, and find the right outside help to keep your thinking fresh, focused and fruitful.

Just like your parents told you all those years ago, it's important to stop, look and listen. Keep yourself and your business safe and strong by getting outside feedback. Most businesses can be helped if issues are caught early enough.

Don't be like the guy mentioned earlier who put off going to the doctor until it was almost too late. Don't allow a lack of action to force your business into being a **Permanent Markdown!**

_____

September/October 2014

Wishin' and Hopin'

◆

If you are of the age that you can claim one-time ownership of a transistor radio, then you might just remember the song "Wishin' and Hopin'." I recently heard this tune while listening to the "oldies" station on my car radio. Ironically, I had just finished speaking with a retailer who had used the exact same words as we discussed his merchandising strategy and year-end outlook. The coincidence really struck me.

Dusty Springfield's catchy tune reached Number 6 on the music's top pop charts in 1964. Though "Wishin' and Hopin'" ("W&H" going forward), is much better suited for a song title than a business strategy, I still encounter many retailers who either fail to plan or who don't effectively implement or execute their plan. These retailers end up with W&H results: Sometimes it works out, most of the time it doesn't.

Planned or Haphazard?

Let me lay out what I mean by the W&H strategy. The W&H retailer typically buys merchandise with no clear thought of how it might fit into the existing assortment. New arrivals are distributed among stores in a predetermined order, and are seldom (if ever) transferred to balance the assortment. This ultimately leads to missed sales opportunities in some stores, while potentially creating unnecessary margin problems in others. In-season markdowns are not addressed in a timely fashion and fill-in orders are hit-and-miss. Promotional merchandise is not sought out regularly, which would help the store build volume and margin. The W&H retailer probably doesn't have solid marketing strategy either. Other typical traits might include not paying attention to freight costs, current market rates on leases, employee selling expenses and inventory shrinkage.

I see this scenario all too often. The W&H merchant enters each new season full of optimism, yet is often left disappointed at season end. The retailer is unprepared to deal with day-to-day reality due to inadequate tools, poor training, lack of time, or insufficient manpower. You can recognize this merchant by his "Ready, Fire, Aim" approach to most problems. This is management by crisis because the day is dominated by the urgent, never leaving time for the important. In other words, valuable time is spent putting out small fires while the big blaze continues to burn out of control. Because of these and other problems, the W&H store is left wishin' for a different outcome than it experienced in the past—*wishin'* customers will like the selections he or she has made and *hopin'* that the store will be profitable at year end. This really isn't much different than playing the lottery. Most of the time, you end up with the same results.

Be Proactive

W&H is a *reactive* strategy, not a proactive one. A goal without a plan to achieve it is nothing more than a wish, and "hope" is not a strategy at all. Many times, a W&H retailer ends up with little or no profit season after season and year after year, barely staying afloat, and not growing or improving. Unfortunately, the vendors and the landlords are the ones making the most money in this case, not the retailer. In some cases, in fact, the retailer is simply buying himself a job.

For better results, make changes now.

If the W&H strategy sounds all too familiar, there are things you can do now to ensure a profitable year. With a full three quarters remaining in the year, there is time to make adjustments to the merchandise plan—but don't put this off. Cash is king in the retail business. With that said:

- Make sure all old merchandise is discounted so that it will be gone by the end of March if possible.

- See that seasonal classifications (i.e., winter boots, slippers, etc.) have realistic stock levels if carryover inventory is needed.

- If you haven't already, review current selections and take markdowns **now** on styles, sizes and colors not performing.

- Any available OTB dollars should be reserved now for fill-ins on key styles and sizes and for opportunistic buys (i.e., off-price).

- Review remaining spring orders to make sure all bases are covered and that you are not out of balance.

- Review operating expenses and make adjustments if expenses look out of line with industry benchmarks.

- Review marketing strategies—including email blasts and social media—for effectiveness.

- Reassess fixtures, signage, lighting, window presentation, and in-store display to determine if updates are warranted.

Perhaps most important of all is to make sure that every employee, beginning with you, is doing everything possible in this competitive retail environment to exceed customer expectations. We all need and want new customers, but it is much easier and less costly to keep existing customers happy and coming back than it is to find new ones.

Make an effort on the items mentioned above and you won't have to go through the rest of this year "Wishin' and Hopin'" for higher profits at year end.

March/April 2014

Enhance the Interaction,
Every Time

◆

Have you ever gone to a rock concert, only to leave feeling the band had simply run through its repertoire of top hits in an effort to get off stage as quickly as possible, collect their fee and get out of town?

Anyone who has been to a Bruce Springsteen concert will concede that what you get is well more than your money's worth. It's not unusual for Springsteen to play shows that are four hours long. The E Street Band always gives 100% and the set list is always different. Bruce Springsteen is an example of an entertainer who clearly exceeds customer expectations.

In today's rapidly changing retail landscape, it is crucial that retailers do everything possible to enhance the consumer experience every time they have a customer interaction, be it in a store or online. As we all know too well, the biggest assortment and the lowest price for anything you want to buy is only a mouse click away. So it's imperative for shoe retailers to, um…put their best foot forward, so to speak.

Attracting new customers is critical to any retailer. However, given that it is "six to seven times more expensive to acquire a new customer than to keep a current one," it is important that we nurture our existing customer relationships. It is also true that news of bad customer service reaches more than twice as many ears as praise for good service. In fact, "it takes twelve positive experiences to make up for one unresolved negative one."

Here's proof. Recently my wife and I were at dinner with a married couple who are friends of ours. The wife had returned that very afternoon from shopping and couldn't wait to unload, in detail, her futile attempt to return an item with tags in place, receipt in hand, and the item still in stock at full price. Since she was admittedly outside the store's return policy, our friend didn't expect a refund, but had hoped for a store credit. Instead, she was told by the "assistant manager" that she was "stuck with it" (she assured us those were the exact words). Access to the store owner to appeal the decision was not possible; consequently, our friend left the store mad and embarrassed, vowing not only never to return, but to post the experience on every social media outlet she could find.

Clearer heads finally prevailed and disaster was averted, but this is the worst possible scenario. This store would have been much better off to grant the store credit, which is what the customer wanted in the first place. This was all over $58. Is it worth it to lose a customer *and* experience all of the potential negative press? Not that this was going to happen, but just imagine how different our dinner conversation might have been if the store employee had graciously asked what she could do to make the customer happy? What if she even included an additional $5 on the store credit just for having to make the extra trip? Today, retailing is all about *exceeding* the customer's expectations.

At the beginning of this year, I asked a few of my clients if they had any stories they could share about good customer service. Here are just a few of the many responses that I received.

- A store owner received a call on Christmas Eve from a customer who was leaving on a ski trip the next morning, but who had forgotten to pick up the skis he had purchased. The owner met him at the store, found the skis, and even went so far as to tell the customer that he could pay the existing balance when they returned from vacation.

- Another store owner hand-delivered presents to her customer on Christmas Eve because, with the customer's husband out of town until Christmas Day, she was needed at home and couldn't get to the store.

- An employee of another client called every husband in her social network, making suggestions on hand-selected gift possibilities; she photographed items on her iPhone so the husbands could take a look, then wrapped the selected gifts and personally delivered them.

- Another client in the Christmas tree business received 700 artificial trees after Thanksgiving (about a month too late, according to my client, and therefore not good). One of the owners personally delivered trees until

10:30 p.m. on a Saturday night in December, because he had promised his customers they would get their trees as soon as they arrived.

- One store owner told an interesting story involving an employee, a certified pedorthist who, while on vacation, delivered a special order to a diabetic customer who lived in a different state.

- One store actually refunded the purchase price of a pair of shoes that was never purchased at the store, simply because the customer was so insistent that it was. Now that really goes above and beyond. Think of the good will created by this gesture—and the negative feelings averted had it been handled differently. The store had every right to decline this refund. Although the manager would have won the battle, he would likely have lost the war.

Another simple step that pays huge dividends is to make sure the people we hire are truly representative of the message we want our customers to receive. The people on the selling floor are the direct face of your business. Always look for people to hire who have friendly, outgoing, gregarious, and warm personalities. I walked into a nationally known home store the other day, walked up to a sales person who looked at me like I was interrupting, didn't smile and made the smallest effort possible to answer my question. I walked out empty-handed. Do you think I will return anytime soon? No, they don't value my business or me as a customer.

The good news here is that bricks-and-mortar retailing still allows us to provide *high touch* service in a *high tech* world. Use your next staff meeting to share examples of how your company has previously exceeded customer expectations and what more can be done in the future.

May/June 2015

The Store Meeting

◆

The store meeting is one of the most important forms of direct communication between owners, managers, buyers, and sales associates. Once a regular part of the work week during the era of mostly full-time employees, this long-held tradition seems to have fallen by the wayside. Taking its place is communication in the form of texts, emails, conference calls, and notices posted by the punch clock or in the break room. Admittedly, the scheduling of store or department meetings is a bit more challenging today than in years past, due to split shifts, days off, vacations, and the increasing use of part-time employees—all of which makes the store meeting that much more necessary.

Timing and Notice

Some stores can get by with regularly scheduled monthly meetings, while others wait for circumstances to dictate a store-wide get-together. Either way, remember to provide ample notice, and pick a time when most employees are able to be present. If store management deems the meeting mandatory, hourly workers need to be compensated for their time, whereas salaried workers do not.

The ideal time for a meeting really depends on the size of the operation. A small store with few employees can perhaps get by with as little as a few minutes on the floor when business is slow. Larger operations will sometimes have meetings before the store opens or after it closes. I work with a particular store that has a storewide meeting every single day, prior to opening, and has done so for years. Store executives would tell you that this form of communication is one of the secrets to their success. They back up their claim with sales exceeding $1,200 per square foot, margins of 55% and a stock turn of four times annually. The meetings are so informative that employees who end up missing a particular meeting—due to a day off or a staggered starting time—feel that they have missed out until they are brought up to speed. Meeting notes are provided to those employees unable to attend.

In multiple store operations, it would be impossible for owners and even buyers to attend each individual store meeting. However, it does lend a feeling of inclusiveness when an owner makes the effort to attend branch store meetings on occasion.

What to Cover

Be sure to keep meetings relevant and positive so that those attending feel that their time is being productively used. There is an array of topics that should be covered regularly, including customer service issues, policies and procedures, shrinkage control, business goals and objectives, sales training techniques, upcoming ads and promotions, and definitely features and benefits of new merchandise arrivals.

What's Hot, What's Not

If you are the meeting organizer, one of your goals will be to get as many people involved in the meeting as practical. Role-playing when dealing with suggestive selling or sales training techniques works well in this situation. Something I have used during meetings is a conversation starter called "What's Hot, What's Not." Each buyer or manager would bring two items to the meeting and be prepared to discuss both. During the "What's Hot" portion, each buyer would share with the group the item that was currently the hottest in the department. This discussion included vendor, quantity purchased, sell through, initial markup, reorder possibilities, how the item was being featured, and just what seemed to make the item so "hot." The procedure was reversed during "What's Not." Buyers would take turns presenting the item that was currently the biggest dog. Discussion points would include why they bought the item, how many they still had, why it was not selling and what they planned to do to move the slow seller. At the end of each buyer's presentation, other buyers and sales associates could offer ideas and suggestions that might prove beneficial.

The "What's Hot, What's Not" discussion was not only entertaining, but also a great learning experience. Each buyer wound up learning what was working and not working, and why, for other buyers and associates in the organization, as well as possible techniques for solving merchandising issues.

Invite Case Studies & Guests

Case studies also make great discussion starters. Have a different employee each meeting bring up an actual issue that has come up for the group to analyze. This promotes group interaction and helps build problem-solving skills. Sales associates can learn from each other the best ways of handling objections as well as complaints.

Another way to make staff meetings interesting is to invite an outside guest. One great idea is to schedule a rep from one of the retailer's major lines to give a "mini-clinic." This is an excellent way for sales associates to hear in detail about the merchandise that the store is or soon will be carrying.

When you return from buying trips, always share new merchandise trends, styles and lines that you have purchased. Your own enthusiasm for the upcoming season's merchandise is contagious—use meetings to share it and pump your employees up.

Involvement Brings Satisfaction

Also, in an effort to get everyone involved, solicit input and invite meeting participants to air minor grievances, as well as possible solutions, or customer comments that affect the store. It's a good idea to monitor this portion of the meeting closely so that it doesn't spiral into a gripe session. Be sure to follow up as quickly as possible on whatever arises. This leads to job satisfaction and employees feeling valued. One way to get everyone involved might be to select a different employee at each meeting to take meeting notes and make sure that everyone, both those in attendance and those that were not, receives a copy.

If you are already conducting regular store meetings, keep doing them. If you are not currently doing so, consider scheduling one soon. Your employees will be very pleased with the open communication.

July/August 2015

"Please Mr. Vendor: Don't Hold a Gun To My Head!"

$\blacklozenge$

A while back I stopped by a local car dealership to check out a car I had seen advertised. The general manager informed me that the particular model I was inquiring about was not allowed to be sold at that location. That seemed odd to me, as the dealership represented only one line of vehicles. So I inquired as to the reason.

I was told that unless the dealership was willing to "invest" money (translation: spend it) to add an additional level onto their building, along with other costly improvements, the dealership would not be allowed to carry the model I was inquiring about. The manager was frustrated by the automobile maker's policy, since he felt his company had always supported this manufacturer through a sizeable inventory investment. Add to that the expense of the existing building and all of the advertising they had paid for over the years to promote the brand and build a customer base. The rules of the game were clearly changing, nobody at the corporate level seemed interested in his concerns, and there was nothing he could do about it. To make matters worse, the manufacturer was spending huge amounts of advertising dollars to generate consumer interest in a vehicle that the dealer wasn't allowed to carry. Feelings of resentment were growing.

Does any of this sound familiar?

I believe most vendors want to provide a good product at a fair price and want the buy/sell relationship to be mutually beneficial. However, certain vendors offer incentives from time to time as coercion to buy other products or lines that they want to sell. I advise retailers not to let vendor incentives, dating, aggressive discounting, threats, intimidation, deadlines, or ultimatums force them into making decisions that are inherently negative for their business. I find it a better business practice to buy products that sell well on their own merits because they are good products.

When incentives must be applied to motivate the buyer to buy, be wary. As a general rule, things do not end well when buying decisions are made under "pressure" circumstances. Below are just a few "sales" techniques you might want to be skeptical of:

- "If you don't increase your order by X% over last year, we will have to offer the line to your competitor."

- "If you don't buy this special program, you won't be considered a 'Five Star' retailer."

- "If you take delivery by X date, you won't have to pay for it until Y date."

- "You have to buy X of specific product in order to maximize marketing dollars."

- "If you don't get the order in by a certain date, you will lose a certain discount/delivery time, or the product might be sold out."

- "If you buy a certain quantity, you will get free freight."

- "We'll even guarantee the sale."

Let's examine these sales ploys more closely and discuss options.

The threat of losing a line to a competitor strikes fear in the hearts of most retailers. It happens all the time anyway, so don't worry about it. Do you really want a vendor thinking that they have that much control over your business? If you feel pressured to concede to this sales tactic, you don't have much of a relationship to begin with. Also, you might as well plan on being bullied again in the future, since it worked this time. ***Course of action:*** *Turn in the order that you feel comfortable with, and let the chips fall where they may.*

In their understandable push for consistency of both product presentation and image, **vendors for years have come up with programs designed to recognize their top dealers.** On the surface, there is nothing at all wrong with this—unless you are striving to become a "Five Star," "Diamond," "Titanium" or some other coveted, precious element dealer *for the wrong* *reasons.* These levels of distinction often are accompanied by perks—greater discounts, return privileges, increased marketing allowance, payment terms, seats on advisory boards, and freight allowances, to name a few. If the size of your orders puts you into this category anyway, fabulous! You deserve the perks, and the dealer recognition is nice. On the other hand, if your ego has taken over your good sense and you are buying more than you should for the sole reason of achieving this distinction, you might want to rethink your priorities. *Course of action: Buy what you can sell, and forget the gratuitous designations unless they make economic sense.*

Oftentimes vendors offer **special dating if you take early delivery.** The pitch is great: Take delivery by such and such a date and you might get several extra months to pay for the merchandise. The idea here is that you will get a longer time in which to sell the product, perhaps even all of it before the invoice is due. Isn't this retail heaven? Not really. Vendors want to keep factories operational and they want the product shipped to you as soon as available for a couple of reasons, primarily: (A) so you won't buy from another resource, and (B) so you can't cancel the order if sales slow because you already have it. The reason I don't care for dating programs is simple: Once the merchandise is received, it begins to sell because of the power of fresh new merchandise. This means the goods you had planned to sell at this time may not sell as quickly, potentially leading to higher markdowns and slower turns. Remember when you are enjoying the extra months that there will be a day of reckoning: the date the invoice is finally due. *Course of action: Though there are numerous exceptions and many cases where dating is favorable, it is best to buy the quantities you want as close to time of need as possible.*

Sometimes you might receive **an extra advertising allowance** if your order reaches a certain level. This just might work for you, because if you have purchased more than you can sell profitably, you will need the extra ad budget for all of the sale ads you will be running. *Course of action: Stick to your open-to-buy plan and buy what you can sell profitably. If you happen to qualify for the advertising allowance, great—but don't reach too far, or the "free" advertising won't be free after all.*

One of my favorites is the enticement of **getting the order turned in by a certain date** or lose a certain discount percentage. Sometimes, you may be told, the product may even be sold out. It takes a lot more than a few discount points to make up for a 50% markdown if you have hastily submitted an order without thorough preparation. Also, I never understood how the product in question could be sold out when there were several more shows left in the selling season. ***Course of action:*** *Take your time, do your homework. If the discount makes sense and you have seen all of the competing lines you need to in the category, pull the trigger.*

In some categories **free freight** is a huge deal and obviously something to be considered. ***Course of action:*** *Know what the savings will be, prior to committing to quantities you can't handle.*

Having a vendor "partner" with you on goods they think you should buy can be a positive. Make certain all parties are clear regarding all terms—including any markdown money, return goods allowances, credits on your account, ending dates, etc. Oftentimes, these programs can leave a retailer with even more slow-moving goods the next season if not executed properly. ***Course of action:*** *Make sure you have a vendor prenuptial agreement prior to embarking a partner program. Get it in writing by someone in authority.*

I am not suggesting that sales incentives aren't worthwhile. They are often very valuable. What I am saying is, don't get greedy. Don't let the "deal" coerce you into making a bad business decision. **Always** ask yourself: Would I be buying this if it wasn't for the particular incentive(s)?

Setting goals and striving to reach them is admirable. However, when achieving a goal benefits one party while putting the other at a disadvantage, the purpose of the relationship comes into question. And the biggest danger that creates is losing the larger objective of mutual benefit to selfish, short-term motivation.

September/October 2015

How to Build a Long-Standing Relationship with Your Bank

◆

To build a long-standing business relationship with a banker, it is important for retailers to understand what the expectations will be, the red flags that can literally kill the deal, how the loan process actually works, and how bankers think.

To begin with, let's examine the ways bankers and independent retailers differ. Typically retailers are entrepreneurs and as such are willing to assume risks in order to succeed. They are for the most part optimistic people focusing on the upside of any given opportunity. Additionally, their businesses are not heavily regulated. When it comes to business growth, "the more, the better" might sum up a retailer's approach. Compare these traits to those of a typical banker. Bankers are by nature risk-avoidant and, generally speaking, pessimistic, choosing to focus on the downside. Banks are highly regulated. They are fine with growth, but take a very conservative approach, wanting to make sure that there is a solid plan in place before committing.

When interviewing a prospective banker for a loan, there are a few questions a **retailer** should ask:

- What is your experience with my industry?

- How does the size of my loan compare with other loans at this bank?

- What happens if I hit a bump in the road?

- Is your bank actively growing its loan portfolio?

- How are loan decisions made at your bank?

- Is the loan officer the decision maker?

- Who will handle my account after closing?

There are also a few questions the banker will ask, so be prepared. The **banker** will want to know how you report financial results. Were they internally prepared? Did a certified public accountant (CPA) review them? Have they been audited? The bank will also inquire as to your ownership structure. Are you a c-corp, s-corp, LLC, or partnership? What does the decision-making process in your organization look like? Do you individually make all the decisions, or are they made by committee, a board or shareholders? The bank will also inquire about your professional providers, including a board of directors, CPA, attorney, or any consultants you might retain for guidance and counsel.

Here are the questions your **bank should** ask you:

- Describe your market.

- Who do you sell to?

- What is your niche?

- What makes your store special or different?

- Who is your competition?

- What are your competitive advantages?

- Describe your financial results and your forecast.

- Where do you see your company in five years?

Bankers like data and information that will back up your request. Here is a partial list of items to provide, preferably before being asked (because volunteering them suggests you have business experience):

- Timely submission of financial statements. Provide a schedule.

- Consistent communication. Let them know they can expect to hear from you regularly.

- Early notification if problems arise. Bankers, for the most part, hate surprises.

- Explanation of large movements in sales, inventory, expenses, etc.

- Budgeting. This could include the income statement and balance sheet, which demonstrate how the business has been performing. Be sure to also include your merchandise plan. A solid sales and inventory forecast shows the banker where you are headed and how you plan to get there.

- Income statements with comparisons to prior periods, including such items as gross margin, owner salaries, depreciation, other non-cash expenses, and one-time non-recurring expenses.

- Pertinent articles from trade magazines are also helpful. Bankers know their industry, but they may need to learn more about yours.

When bankers review your numbers, they focus on three main areas. The first is **collateral**—in other words, how much you are willing to put in. You must have "skin in the game." The other two areas are **cash flow** and **financial strength**—which is to say, liquidity and capital.

Red Flags for a Bank

Be forewarned of the areas that send up the red flag for the bank. If not overcome, these are potential deal killers:

- No budget. This should be obvious. Don't waste your time, or the banker's, without one. All you will end up with is a free cup of coffee and a complimentary pen with the bank's logo on it.

- Poor credit score or no credit references.

- Lack of understanding or inability to explain your own numbers.

- Complicated ownership structure.

- Tax income that looks very different than book income.

- Your primary concern is what the interest rate will be and/or if you will have to sign a personal guarantee.

- A belief that the loan can be paid back through profits alone.

- No management team.

- Expansion and growth without proper planning.

- Inability to provide periodic and timely financial information.

- Slowing turnover. This is a big sign that inventory is growing faster than sales, and is an indication of potential cash flow and margin concerns.

- No "skin in the game." (Yes, I mentioned this before, but it's worth repeating.)

- Poor communication or lack of honesty.

- Fighting with management, between partners, or among family members.

For starters, your banker will request two years of income tax returns for the company and each owner, and two years of financials, along with interim financials for the current year. You might also be asked for a personal financial statement and an accounts receivable and accounts payable aging report.

Don't be surprised by a request for a personal guarantee. An unwillingness to put personal funds into a business, should they be necessary, sends a strong message to the loan review committee. Although retailers don't normally like the idea of being personally liable, bankers often feel a need to look at an owner's personal credit as well as his business credit, for one simple reason: If the owner is not willing to put in personally for his business, why should the bank?

Finally, the importance of positive cash flow cannot be overstated. The lack of cash flow kills more deals right from the beginning than almost anything else.

Assuming that you have made it this far, here is what the loan evaluation process entails. The bank will pull your credit report. Some banks key in on particular data points from the information collected to come up with what might be called a "liquid credit score." If the LCS comes in above their base requirements, they will most likely move forward with the loan review process. From there, the bank reviews the data for business and personal cash flow to be certain you won't experience any difficulty making the loan payments. Once all of the other factors previously mentioned have been reviewed and all are deemed satisfactory, the collateral requirements will be established.

Understanding how banks think and operate, along with being prepared, will go a long way toward successful loan approval and a longstanding banking relationship.

November/December 2015

You Can't Manage
What You Don't Measure

◆

In the game of golf, everything is measured. The total individual score is measured against par. This measurement is so vital to the game that players are actually provided a card on which to record the number of times they hit the ball, known as "strokes taken." Some golfers are obsessed with tracking other statistics of the game in hopes of discovering shortcomings in need of improvement. Areas sometimes analyzed include length of drives, number of drives that reach the fairway, greens in regulation, and number of putts required to get the ball in the hole.

Runners log total miles run. Weightlifters chart progress by keeping journals of amount of weight lifted and number of repetitions performed. Some of the more dedicated ones even track calories and monitor food portions during the day in an effort to manage progress. The point of all this is evident to athletes: Without benchmark information as a reference point, you don't know where you need to improve. How can you be expected to know what is good if you aren't sure what is bad?

Retail Is Detail

In the retail business, there are numerous areas that require measurement in order to achieve success. Sales volume is the obvious starting point. All retailers want to know how they did compared to last year, last month, last Saturday. Great care must be taken to make sure that the comparison is valid. For example, if last year's sales were driven by markdowns and this year's volume for the same time period came in lower, it is possible that the sales you had were more profitable than the preceding year. Other important considerations to keep in mind when measuring sales include the weather, the timing of certain holidays from year to year, and various promotions that may have occurred.

All retailers have a pretty good idea of where they stand on sales for a given period. There are, however, several other merchandising benchmark numbers that require measuring lest they fail to get the management attention that they deserve. This list includes, but is not limited to, operating expenses, markdowns, shrinkage, initial and maintained markups, merchandise-on-order, and open-to-buy.

Operating Expenses

Operating expenses for some retailers can account for as much as 43 cents out of every dollar sold. They should be planned out by line item and reviewed periodically. Rent, payroll, advertising, even insurance and interest costs may be more controllable than you think. Compare your expenses against those in your industry and make sure you are within an acceptable range.

Markdowns

I am often surprised to find retailers that do not know how many markdowns they have taken. It is impossible to manage something if you have no starting point. Track markdowns by vendor and classification, at the very least. Remember that markdowns are expressed as a percentage of sales. Capturing markdown information by style and size may also prove beneficial. Most, though not all, computer POS systems do an adequate job of tracking markdown information.

Shrinkage

Inventory shrinkage is another area to which some retailers don't seem to pay much attention. This comes right off the profit line. If the difference between your book and physical inventory is outside of industry norms, start asking questions and tighten things up.

Markups

Review initial and maintained markups on a regular basis. Initial markups need to be sufficient enough to cover markdowns and operating expenses, and to satisfy profit requirements. The web is a great resource to research just about anything. A random internet check of styles you carry will let you know if you are selling at competitive prices. Industry associations often publish typical ranges of maintained markup and gross margin figures, which enable you to gauge your operation against norms.

Try this: Calculate how the merchandise you have on order for the next season stacks up against your projected sales.

Here is a simple test that I use with my clients all the time. Take the on-hand retail inventory of a given classification. Add to that the merchandise on-order you have committed to for the upcoming season. Don't forget to estimate for any size fill-ins or reorders that you think you might need. Subtract the estimated sales you expect, as well as the amount of markdowns you feel might be reasonable.

Compare the ending number you get with your inventory plan. If you are not happy with what you come up with, you have a few options: you can adjust orders, promote earlier, hope business is better than you planned, pray, or do nothing at all and suffer the consequences of having too much inventory at the end of the season.

Measuring, analyzing, and adjusting these and other quantifiable areas of your business will help you do two essential things: fine-tune the expectations you have of your staff, and create a winning strategy.

January/February 2016

Acknowledgments

◆

I am grateful to several individuals for their help, as well as for their guidance, inspiration, and dedication. First and foremost is my uncle, Don Sayner, who as a buyer for several major department stores sparked my interest in the retail business at a very young age and mentored me along the way. I am also grateful for the opportunity I was given by the late Samuel Fellows who, as president of the Wm. Doerflinger Company in LaCrosse, Wisconsin, allowed an enthusiastic eighteen-year-old kid—me—the chance to be his men's buyer and department manager. Thanks to my parents for instilling in me a solid work ethic and making me stick to everything I started. Credit also goes to my wife, Sandra, for her inspira-tion and input. She is the first to read everything I write, and she provides me with a much appreciated critical eye. I would also like to acknowledge the National Shoe Retailers Association (NSRA), which has provided me with a forum to share my experiences, especially *Shoe Retailing Today* editor Nancy Hultquist. My gratitude also extends to my colleagues at RMSA, who to me represent the greatest collection of retail knowledge ever assembled. Special recognition goes out to Michael Adams who added me to the RMSA team.

I'd like also to extend a special thank you to the many retailers past and present with whom I have worked: I have learned from you, and continue to do so every day. This book would not be possible without you.

About the Author

◆

Ritchie Sayner began his retail career in 1969 at Wm. Doerflinger Co., a department store in LaCrosse, Wisconsin. Two years later, at the age of eighteen, he was named menswear buyer and was thought to be the youngest buyer in the country at the time. He was promoted to merchandise manager at the age of twenty-three, with responsibility for ten buyers. While holding this position, Sayner became a certified instructor and taught principles of retailing, salesmanship, and merchandise management. He is a graduate of the University of Wisconsin-LaCrosse, where he majored in marketing.

Since 1980, Sayner has been employed by RMSA, a retail consulting firm headquartered in Riverside, California. He volunteers for SCORE, consulting with retailers around the country. During his free time, he is on a golf course as often as possible. He has two grown children and four grandchildren, and currently lives in Kansas City, Missouri, with his wife and their two cats.

Contact rsayner@rmsa.com or visit online at www.write4retail.com and www.facebook.com/RitchieSayner.